S·U·P·E·R·C·A·R·S

FERRARI TESTAROSSA

MARK HUGHES

GALLERY BOOKS
An Imprint of W. H. Smith Publishers Inc.
112 Madison Avenue
New York City 10016

A SALAMANDER BOOK

This 1988 edition published by Gallery Books,
an imprint of
W.H. Smith Publishers Inc.,
112 Madison Avenue,
New York, New York 10016

and

W.H. Smith Canada Ltd.,
York House,
113 Merton Street,
Toronto,
Canada M4S 1A8

ISBN 0-8317-3211-3

All correspondence concerning the content of this
volume should be addressed to Salamander Books
Ltd., 52 Bedford Row, London WC1R 4LR, United
Kingdom.

This volume not for sale outside the United States
of America and Canada

Editor: Richard Collins

Designer: Paul Johnson

Line diagrams: Keith Palmar
(© Salamander Books Ltd)

Colour profiles: Stephen Seymour
(© Salamander Books Ltd)

Filmset by Technotype Ltd

Colour reproduction by Scantrans, Singapore

Printed in Hong Kong

Acknowledgements

Research into this book would have been
impossible without the tremendous help provided
by many people at Maranello, most notably *Dottore*
Pietro de Franchi and *Ingegnere* Maurizio Rossi. At
Pininfarina, Daniela Cappa and Aldo Brovarone
were most generous in their assistance. I am also
grateful to several people at Maranello
Concessionaires, Egham, Surrey, particularly
Shaun Bealey (formerly Deputy Chairman), Peter
Whittle and Nick Stevens. Keith Hopkins of KBH,
Ferrari's public relations agency in Britain, gave
me my first opportunity to drive a Testarossa.

Contents

FERRARI'S SUPERCAR HERITAGE   4

DESIGN AND DEVELOPMENT   14

TESTAROSSA DISSECTED   24

MANUFACTURE   40

DRIVING IMPRESSIONS   54

INDEX   64

INTRODUCTION

Over the whole spectrum of automotive history, no car manufacturer has drawn more clichés and purple prose than Ferrari. All the products of its forty-one years can be labelled supercars, but some have risen to greater heights than others.

In recent memory, one year – 1984 – stands out as a landmark in Ferrari progress. In the space of a few months, two of the greatest road cars ever to emerge from Maranello were launched to the public. One was the 'homologation special' GTO, a limited run of 272 cars embracing Grand Prix technology in its lightweight carbon-fibre and Kevlar construction, its 400bhp twin-turbocharged 2.9-litre V8 engine and its formidable cornering power. The other was the Testarossa, a supercar in a quite different vein with a similarly exotic specification.

Whereas the GTO was a pragmatic production special built in one batch to fulfil the needs of a stillborn racing programme, the Testarossa was Ferrari's supercar flagship for the 1980s, a machine designed to carry the company towards the twenty-first century. It took the already legendary capabilities of the Berlinetta Boxer a stage further in becoming a refined racing car for the road.

Its 5-litre flat-12 engine, derived directly from competition experience, sits behind the two-seat cockpit and delivers 390bhp, enough to push the car to a top speed of 180mph. It has incredible handling, gorgeous Pininfarina styling and a vivid personality. So many wealthy people around the world aspire to owning one that there is an extremely long waiting list.

Ever since the fuel crisis of the early 1970s, the future of supercars has seemed precarious. Several great cars – Maserati, Jensen and de Tomaso – fell by the wayside in those bleak days, but Ferrari shrugged off pessimism about the future by investing heavily in modernising its factory. The company has blossomed through the 1980s, the Testarossa spearheading its progress, to become larger than ever before.

Whether or not the future is bright for supercars, the Ferrari Testarossa will stand as one of the truly outstanding cars of our time. Charismatic, fast, beautiful and . . . not quite perfect . . . it is everything that a supercar should be.

FERRARI'S SUPERCAR HERITAGE

All Ferraris are supercars but some of the Testarossa's forebears stand out from this exclusive pack

THE MODERN TESTAROSSA'S ROOTS go back to the very beginnings of Ferrari, just after World War II. The tenets of Ferrari's philosophy have never changed, for the Testarossa is a product of the same set of inspirational factors which resulted in the first roadgoing 166 models.

Ferrari has always striven to make its road cars as near as possible in performance, handling and braking to its racing machinery, and this ethos has held good in every car the company has ever made. Some cars have been more compromised than others for the sake of refinement and practicality, but there has never been a mundane Ferrari. And, despite the growing performance constraints imposed by modern motoring, there never will be.

'Racing improves the breed' is one of the commonest automotive maxims, and Ferrari has followed this faith implicitly. Every one of its remarkable road cars, right to its present day range, embraces engineering developed on the world's race circuits. Ferrari is unique among post-war car makers in having an unbroken involvement in Formula 1 racing, and its sports car racing activities continued uninterrupted until 1973. No wonder every car that Ferrari has ever made can rightly be judged a supercar.

TWELVE CYLINDERS
Post-war advances
Enzo Ferrari began to produce his first cars in 1947, astonishingly only two years after the end of the war. Most other manufacturers in Europe and the USA were gingerly returning to full-scale production with crudely modernised versions of their pre-war offerings, yet here was Ferrari, virtually a complete novice in the business, producing machines which were startlingly and refreshingly new. Given a few more years, other manufacturers – like Jaguar, with its sensational XK120 – would produce new models, but none would move with Ferrari's speed or daring.

What made Ferrari even more special, indeed unique, was the audacity of his designs. Not for him a conservative approach with simply engineered cars. He took the plunge straight away with a complex new V12 engine, a decision which created a twelve-cylinder bloodline surviving to this day.

Before the war, V12s had been comparatively common among exclusive car manufacturers seeking the highest levels of mechanical smoothness and relaxed power. In the USA, Cadillac, Lincoln and Packard, to name just a few, produced V12-engined cars – these were the days when the USA led the automotive world in sophistication. In Europe, Hispano-Suiza, Lagonda, Rolls-Royce and Daimler all sought the refinement which only a twelve-cylinder engine could provide.

By 1947, however, only Lincoln remained, and it too was shortly to abandon its V12. Economical manufacture required a simpler approach for the imminent post-war boom, but Enzo Ferrari remained a maverick in his thinking. Throughout the 1950s and well into the 1960s, Ferrari would be alone in offering a V12 as the ultimate badge of exclusivity.

Today, the V12 has returned. Lamborghini led the pack which began to snap at Ferrari's heels when it introduced a V12 in 1964 for the 350GT, to be followed by the Miura, Islero, Espada, Jarama and Countach succession of models. Jaguar fitted its new V12 to the E-type in 1971, following this with the XJ12 saloon a year later; this engine is commonly recognised as the silkiest V12 even today. Far more recently, in 1987, BMW created a V12 (after a decade of gestation) for its 750i saloon flagship, and arch-rivals Mercedes-Benz plan to follow suit. Despite the fuel crisis of the mid-1970s and the recession of the early 1980s, the V12 is slowly making a return to the pre-eminence it enjoyed fifty years ago. Whether the new lease of life will prove to be only temporary remains to be seen.

Some consider the 275GTB the most beautiful of Ferraris, others find its styling rather heavy. But it is undeniably one of the greatest, whether in two-cam or four-cam specification. First shown in Paris in 1964, it introduced two new features – all-independent suspension and a transaxle gearbox – derived from Ferrari's racing experience. Its 3286cc V12 engine produced 280bhp, enough to take the car to over 150mph. The 300bhp four-cam, shown here, arrived in 1966, establishing a new standard of power/capacity; a standard which Ferrari has yet to beat with its naturally-aspirated road cars

But Ferrari led the trend. Throughout the Maranello company's history, there have always been twelve-cylinder cars in its model line-up. Indeed, Enzo Ferrari has often said that a real Ferrari *must* have twelve cylinders. He has had this commitment to twelve cylinders, to watch-like engineering precision, ever since the 1920s, when his infatuation is said to have been nurtured by examining a Packard owned by the lady Italian racing driver, the Baroness Maria Antonietta Avanzo.

The nucleus of the engineering team Ferrari assembled around him comprised Luigi Bazzi and Gioacchino Colombo, both of whom had worked pre-war for Scuderia Ferrari, the operation which ran works Alfa Romeos in motor racing on the factory's behalf (rather as Tom Walkinshaw masterminds Jaguar's racing programme today). Although Bazzi had worked almost continuously for Ferrari since the early 1920s, Colombo returned to his fold in 1946 to take up the position of chief engineer.

Colombo immediately began work on a V12 which could be used, with some modification, for Ferrari's entire programme of Grand Prix, sports racing and road car manufacture. Although Ferrari intended to start with a Grand Prix car, the sports racing version appeared first, handled by Franco Cortese in a minor race at Piacenza on 11 May 1947. The car led the race but failed to finish, but a fortnight later Cortese gave the new Ferrari marque its first win at the Caracalla circuit in Rome.

Unlike the big V12s which had inspired Ferrari, Colombo's design was a tiny unit displacing just 1497cc. It laid the design foundations from which all twelve-cylinder Ferraris have originated. Its two banks of cylinders were inclined at 60° and a bore and stroke of 55mm × 52.5mm gave slightly over-square cylinder dimensions. Power was given initially as 118bhp at 6500rpm, but it would climb

dramatically as Colombo produced many permutations – some of them supercharged – from his basic building block.

Many aspects of this V12's specification continue to the present Testarossa. The crankcase and detachable cylinder heads were made from silumin light alloy, and cast iron liners were shrunk in. The high resistance steel crankshaft was supported on seven main bearings, carrying con rods and pistons in pairs. The two camshafts sat on the top of the blocks and were driven by automatically-tensioned chains to actuate inclined valves; the Testarossa has four camshafts driven by rubber belts and four valves per cylinder, but the principles haven't changed.

Following a practice which he would use until the 1970s, Ferrari designated Colombo's first V12 the 125, the number indicating the capacity of one cylinder – one-twelfth of 1.5 litres. The basic design quickly grew to types 166 (1992cc), 195 (2340cc), 212 (2563cc), 225 (2715cc) and 250 (2963cc), and even beyond this. Throughout this 'expansion programme', the stroke remained fixed at the 166's 58.8mm, each displacement increase being achieved simply by pulling out the bore diameter.

There were limiting factors in Colombo's design – chiefly its siamesed intake porting which limited the amount of valve overlap that could be worked into any camshaft design – which meant that Ferrari sought a second basic V12 concept. Following Colombo's return to Alfa Romeo in 1949, his successor as Ferrari's chief engineer, Aurelio Lampredi (then only 30 years old), set to work on a larger V12 which would be used chiefly in competition.

Although it retained the general concept of Colombo's 60° single-cam V12, it featured bore centre spacings of 108mm (instead of the Colombo V12's 90mm) to allow for larger bore diameters; consequently, Lampredi's engine became known

as the 'long block' V12. Its major design departure lay in having integral cylinder heads, which solved head/block sealing problems but made engine overhauls far more time-consuming.

With such a slender dividing line between Ferrari's early competition and road models, perhaps the 342 America 2+2 styled by Ghia should be considered its first true road car. Few of these 4.1-litre cars with all-synchromesh four-speed gearboxes were built, but they led on to a line of Lampredi-engined cars running through the 375 America, 410 Superamerica and 400 Superamerica, culminating in 1964 with the 500 Superfast, a true luxury limousine. As a background to the Testarossa, however, our attention should be confined to Ferrari's ultimate supercars.

THE 250GT SERIES
Early growth
An incredible number of road Ferraris, with a bewildering succession of type numbers, have played their part in Maranello's supercar heritage, but the beginning of proper volume production came with the 250GT launched in 1956 at the Geneva Show.

Over five years, nearly 500 of these were built, all using a Colombo single-cam V12 engine displacing 2953cc from a 73mm bore and 58.8mm stroke. Three twin-choke Weber carburettors gave a power output of 240bhp at 7000rpm. Early convertible models were designed and built by Boano, but in 1958 came the Scaglietti-built 250GT California with delicious Pininfarina styling. Pininfarina was also responsible for the coupé bodies which made up the bulk of 250GT production.

Ferrari made its first concession to the family man by introducing the 250GT 2+2 (often known also as the 250GTE) in 1960. Its two rear seats were inadequate for adults, but small children were quite happy in them. These cars, although sharing

the mechanical specification of other 250GTs, don't stand as high in Ferrari's road car reputation because of their softer character, but a production run of around 900 made them very popular in their day.

Apart from the competition-oriented 250GT SWB (short wheelbase) and 250GTO, the great classic of the 250GT line was the Berlinetta Lusso (meaning luxury). All the way from its low-slung nose, through its airy glass area to the descending sweep of its tail, the Lusso's graceful Pininfarina lines have an irresistible beauty which, in the eyes of many beholders, surpasses all other Ferraris. It is one of the most seductive cars the world has ever seen. Around 350 Lussos were built at Sergio Scaglietti's Modena bodyshop down the road from Maranello, each one painstakingly crafted by hand.

275GTB
Dramatic advances

The gorgeous Lusso was discontinued in late 1964, and replaced by the 275GTB (Gran Turismo Berlinetta). This new model, still following Ferrari's cylinder capacity designation, featured an enlarged engine of 3.3 litres.

Ferrari made dramatic advances in its supercar production specification with the 275GTB, breaking with what had become a tradition of conservative mechanical design. Among the most significant features to make their first appearance on a Ferrari road car were all-independent suspension and a combined rear-mounted gearbox and final drive unit, commonly known as a transaxle.

Both of these concepts had been developed on sports racing and single-seater machines, so actually there was nothing outlandish about the 275GTB. The rear-mounted transmission's fine pedigree in competition reached back to the days of the 1950s Formula 1 and 2 cars with De Dion rear suspension, as well as the Mondial and Monza sports cars. Testa Rossa sports racers of 1958 also used rear-mounted gearboxes in conjunction with De Dion suspension, but then reverted to a new 'all-indirect' (meaning there was no direct drive, with a pair of gears always involved in transmitting drive) five-speed gearbox design placed conventionally in line with the engine. This 'all-indirect' unit, which remained in use on all Ferrari's sports racers until the rear-engined era, was the basis of the 275GTB's transaxle, although it required new external castings to adapt it to the adjacent final drive.

The rear suspension mated to this transaxle system was independent, for the first time on a Ferrari road car. Its layout of parallel wishbones, coil spring/damper units and an anti-roll bar was derived from the 250LM rear-engined sports racer – the spring/damper units, extending upwards from the outer ends of the upper wishbones, protruded high into the body. The front suspension followed similar double wishbone principles, except that the spring/damper units were attached to the lower wishbones and fitted through the upper ones.

In departing from the 250 powerplant's well-known dimensions of 73mm × 58.8mm, the 275 engine achieved 3286cc by enlarging the bore to 77mm. As installed in a standard 275GTB, this engine gave 280bhp at 7500rpm, but higher states of tune could be specified by customers: for example, there was a model labelled the 275GTB/C with six Weber carburettors in place of the standard trio of twin-choke 40DCL6 Webers, as well as dry sump lubrication and alloy body panels. The 275GTS (Spyder) version, a slightly less

overtly sporting car, came in a lower state of tune, developing 260bhp at 7500rpm on a 9.3:1 compression ratio.

A new engine with four overhead camshafts in late 1966 turned the 275GTB into one of the all-time great supercars. Designated the 275GTB/4, this car produced 300bhp at 8000rpm and 202lb ft of torque at 5500rpm, making the earlier models seem relatively ordinary. This prodigious power was quite remarkable for a 3.3-litre engine, giving a specific power output of 91.3bhp per litre – no subsequent naturally-aspirated production Ferrari has exceeded this.

Pininfarina's design for the 275GTB wasn't one of its best, since the car's chunky appearance and relatively small glass area was a little dated when measured against the crisper, sharp-edged shapes that were beginning to appear. Its bulbous lines, with cowled headlamps and a wraparound

windscreen accentuating its bold curves, were attractive enough, but in no way avant-garde.

But shape is only a small part of any supercar's make-up, and the 275GTB's mechanical excellence allows it to stand high in Ferrari ratings. Indeed, there are experienced Ferrari owners who rate the ultimate 275GTB, the four-cam GTB/4, as superior to the Daytona which followed it, with equally formidable performance and even more progressive handling.

DAYTONA
Consummate beauty

The relatively cool response received by the 275GTB, as well as the advances being made by rival manufacturers, like Lamborghini with its Miura, required a dramatic solution from Ferrari. The car commissioned from Pininfarina in late 1966 was all that it needed to be, even though its

Nowadays the best place to extend a Ferrari is on the track, as one 275GTB owner finds at Donington, *above left*. The 365GTB/4, *below left*, commonly known as the Daytona, is probably the most revered of all Ferrari's road cars, commanding staggering prices today; the best examples cost twice as much as a new Testarossa. Ferrari was inspired by the design of its Formula 1 cars when the 365GT4 BB, *above*, or Berlinetta Boxer, appeared with a 4390cc (the same capacity as the Daytona) flat-12 engine mounted behind the cockpit

basic configuration – front-mounted engine driving the rear wheels – looked positively traditional compared with the Miura's transversely-set mid-mounted V12, or even Ferrari's own mid-engined baby supercar, the 246 Dino.

This new supercar was the stunning 365GTB/4, popularly known as the Daytona. The name was inspired by Ferrari's success in the 1967 Daytona 24-Hours, when Maranello made up for its defeat by Ford at the previous year's Le Mans 24-Hours by staging a 1-2-3 formation finish with two of its new P4 sports racers and an older P3. The Daytona name came to be used as an in-house designation during pre-production development – the title was adopted by the press in describing the new car, even though it always bore only 365GTB/4 badging.

The Daytona must be one of the most sensational supercars of all time. Its body, styled once again by Pininfarina, is a timeless combination of curves and straight edges. It was not universally admired at the time of its launch at the Paris Salon in October 1968, but few people question its consummate beauty today. Twenty years on, its thrusting nose, graceful coupé cabin and tidy tail treatment remain thoroughly modern. Despite its size (kerb weight is 3442lb), its styling purity contrives to give it perfect proportions. Few cars have such a powerful presence.

Looks aren't everything, and the Daytona's enduring appeal – it has blossomed to become the most collectible of all series production Ferraris, comfortably commanding six-figure prices today – lies in its formidable specification. And this, of course, starts with its V12 engine, which reached new levels of sophistication.

Ferrari chose a 4390cc V12 with four overhead camshafts, like the 275GTB/4. The bore was taken to 81mm, the stroke to 71mm, and the compression ratio was set at 9.3:1. Six twin-choke Weber 40DCN21 carburettors filling the 60° vee were specified for European models, and in this form the V12 delivered a massive 352bhp at 7500rpm and 315lb ft of torque at 5500rpm. A pair of inclined valves sat in each hemispherical combustion chamber, with a single spark plug mounted between them. Following established practice, the crankshaft, machined from a single steel casting, ran in seven main bearings, with each throw carrying con rods and pistons connected up in pairs.

As with its other all-aluminium V12s, Ferrari used wet cylinder liners in cast iron. So large were the cylinders that adjacent liners touched each other, this siamesing bringing them into direct contact with cooling water. There were two distributors mounted on the tail end of each

7

exhaust camshaft, and a large aluminium timing cover housed the water pump and two camshaft chain drives. Dry sump lubrication was employed, incorporating two scavenge pumps and a pressure pump.

Power was transmitted through a single-plate clutch to a torque tube drive-line – comprising a propshaft enclosed within a rigid steel tube – extending to the transaxle gearbox. This arrangement fixed the relative positions of engine and transmission, whose torsional movements with load and lift-off were countered by a torque-reaction rod to enhance drive-line smoothness. The greatest benefit of this transaxle configuration, derived from the 275GTB, was near-perfect weight distribution.

Suspension followed the 275GTB's example in being independent front and rear, with exactly the same parallel wishbone arrangement. Like the 275GTB, the rear spring/damper units sat above the upper wishbones to feed loads into tall fabricated turrets. To match the Daytona's awesome performance, the braking system was very powerful – discs front and rear, with four-pot calipers bearing on them. The bodywork was constructed largely of steel, with aluminium for unstressed panels like bonnet, boot lid and doors.

The Daytona's launch came soon after the first batch of mild safety and exhaust emissions regulations were introduced in the USA. Although the 275GTB/4 was unable to meet the new rules, a federal version of the Daytona was available from the beginning to keep a Ferrari flagship in this important market. The American specification included a lowered compression ratio of 8.8:1 to allow the engine to run on low octane fuel without detonation problems, and a massive power-strangling exhaust silencer box sitting in a revised system. The more usual Daytona frontal treatment, with solid headlamp covers instead of the transparent plexiglass panels seen on early models, was also a federal requirement.

Although fifteen years have passed since the last Daytona was made, it remains one of the fastest supercars the world has ever seen. Few road Ferraris have been independently tested by magazines over the years, but Paul Frère was able to obtain figures for the Daytona, thanks largely to his special position as a former Ferrari works racing driver.

Despite his rather precarious procedure of validating the Daytona's top speed on public *autostradas*, Frère eventually found a stretch of road quiet enough to achieve a mean maximum speed (the average of two runs in opposite directions) of 175.7mph (282.7kmh). To give a measure of this achievement (for a *1960s* car, remember), the fastest car *Autocar* has ever tested is a Lamborghini Countach 5000 at 178mph, and this was only in 1985. The next nearest maximum is 162mph for a Porsche 911 Turbo 3.3 tested in 1983.

Frère's Daytona acceleration figures were 0–60mph in 5.8sec (4.8sec for the 911 Turbo 3.3), 0–100mph in 12.8sec (11.5sec) and 0–140mph in 24.6sec (25.5sec). While the Daytona was slightly slower than the Porsche until 130mph, from there on its superior aerodynamics gave it the edge.

Some owners criticised the Daytona for its heavy steering and unwieldy handling in town driving, but this is the wrong environment in which to judge the car. For fast, long-distance, open road journeys it was without peer. Taking a Daytona above 100mph put it in its happiest element: at three-figure speeds, its steering weight, ride suppleness and balanced handling were almost perfect.

Although most Daytonas were coupés, a highly exclusive spyder (the 365GTS/4) was also made. Factory production of these numbered fifty, but many coupés have subsequently had their tops chopped off – these 'after-market' conversions, however, are nowhere near as valuable today as the real thing.

While the 275GTB had been intended very much as a road car, it was inevitable that the Daytona's staggering performance would be put to good use in sports car racing's GT category. Fifteen pure competition Daytonas, skinned entirely in aluminium and glass-fibre, were built at Maranello in three series. The first series used standard mechanical running gear; the second series used tuned engines delivering 402bhp in lightened cars weighing 400lb less than standard; and the third series took power to 450bhp and featured modified suspension.

Privateers raced these cars intensively with factory support, and their best showing came at Le Mans in 1972. Out of nine cars entered, five took the top places in their class, finishing between fifth and ninth overall against proper prototype opposition. The Daytona was never intended as a competition car, but showed its pedigree tremendously well when put to the ultimate test.

BERLINETTA BOXER
Born from Formula 1
While the Daytona concluded a logical evolution from the very first V12 Ferraris in its traditional configuration of front engine driving rear wheels, the Berlinetta Boxer which arrived in 1971 was very different. The new car had its engine positioned behind the cockpit, and for the first time it featured twelve cylinders laid out in horizontally opposed (180°) formation.

That 'racing improves the breed' philosophy was responsible for the change, since Formula 1 cars had had their engines mounted behind the driver for ten years. The Boxer, however, was not the first roadgoing mid-engined Ferrari, since the layout had been pioneered by the Dino(first with 206 and then 246 versions of its V6 engine) in 1968. Despite not being badged as a Ferrari initially, and to this day remaining relatively unaccepted by true *Ferraristi*, the Dino showed the immense handling advantages which could be obtained by concentrating mass towards the centre of the car.

While the Daytona's road behaviour was as exceptional as its performance, the weight split of engine at the front and transaxle at the rear could create a dumb-bell handling effect in extreme circumstances, encouraging a spin when the car was near the limit. Few drivers were ever likely to push a Daytona this far, but the fact that the car was conceptually outdated needed rectification. Since Lamborghini, with its mid-engined Miura, had usurped Ferrari in the vanguard of innovation and progress, Maranello had to fight back with its own interpretation of the ultimate mid-engined car. The Daytona could have continued for many years, but the exclusive buying public, thought Ferrari, might begin to perceive it as being too traditional.

The 365GT4 BB, as the new car was labelled, had one thing in common with the Daytona – although its flat-12 engine was completely different in concept, its capacity of 4390cc was identical. Indeed, many Daytona V12 components, such as pistons and con rods, were carried over to the new design, illustrating the evolutionary commonsense which has always pervaded Maranello. Carburation, as always, was provided by an arsenal of Webers, four triple-choke units being standard wear for the Boxer. Power rose

Launched in the same year as the Testarossa, the GTO is a thinly veiled competition car, having been designed for a Group B endurance racing category which never materialised. Rules required that 200 cars had to be built for Group B eligibility, but so desirable was the GTO, with its twin-turbocharged 2855cc V8 engine, that 272 were eventually made

fractionally higher than the Daytona's 352bhp, to 360bhp at 7000rpm. This was accompanied by a slightly reduced torque figure of 311lb ft at 4500rpm.

The Boxer's lines were a strong statement of aggressive beauty. Pininfarina – who else? – somehow blended the Dino's seductive curvaceousness with the Daytona's restrained brutality

to produce an entirely new shape which could be nothing but a Ferrari. This sensitivity to evolutionary form is the key to Pininfarina's sublime ability, a talent which has ensured that it has remained Maranello's leading stylist since 1952.

Considering the inherent impracticalities of a mid-engined layout, the Boxer didn't do too badly in day-to-day driving. The low flat-12 allowed good rearward visibility, even if the almost total lack of luggage space was a severe black mark compared with the Daytona. As a true racing car for the road, the Boxer set remarkable standards of ride comfort, noise refinement and docility, requiring less physical effort from its driver than a Daytona.

Its performance was almost exactly on a par with the Daytona's – marginally quicker up to 80mph, but thereafter slightly slower to the factory's claimed top speed of 181.0mph (291.3kmh). To quote Frère's figures once again, the 365GT4 BB achieved 0–60mph in 5.4sec, 0–100mph in 13.0sec and 0–140mph in 26.5sec. His top speed of 172.8mph (278.1kmh) was slightly down on the factory's figure.

After 387 365GT4 BBs had been produced,

Ferrari was forced to update the Boxer in 1976 to meet new European noise and pollution regulations. Since mere amendment of the 4.4-litre engine would have sacrificed too much power, capacity rose to 4942cc by increasing the bore from 81mm to 82mm, and the stroke from 72mm to 78mm. Even so, power dropped to 340bhp at 6200rpm, although the engine's torque curve was flattened to provide even better flexibility and responsiveness, the peak rising from the 4.4-litre engine's 311lb ft to 331lb ft at 4300rpm. Dry sump lubrication was also added to counter the oil surge likely to be caused by the even greater cornering forces possible with the 512BB, as the car became known.

Performance tailed off slightly, the factory giving a new top speed of 176.0mph (283.2kmh) and fractionally longer acceleration times – but no owner was ever able to tell the difference. To answer criticism of the 365GT4 BB's tendency to become unstable at high speeds in strong winds, a spoiler was added to the 512BB's chin. There were other subtle bodywork modifications, most notably a pair of NACA ducts on the flanks to direct air to the rear brakes.

The Testarossa's predecessor was the 512BB, fitted first with Weber carburettors and then with Bosch K-Jetronic fuel injection. A pair of NACA ducts fitted ahead of the rear wheels distinguish the 4942cc 512 Boxer from the 4390cc 365

The final development of the Boxer line was to add Bosch K-Jetronic fuel injection in February 1982 to create the 512BBi, with flexibility enhanced still further. All the time Ferrari was moving towards the refinement that its ever more exclusive market demanded, no longer putting ultimate power at the top of its requirements. Power stayed the same at 340bhp, although it was developed slightly lower down the scale at 6600rpm – torque rose by a whisker to 333lb ft at 4200rpm.

By now Ferrari had arrived gently at the threshold of the Testarossa's specification. The new car, launched in 1984, would not make as great a technical leap as the Boxer, but it would take Ferrari a few more rungs up the supercar ladder . . .

THE OTHER TESTA ROSSA
The first redhead

The current Testarossa isn't the first Ferrari to bear this evocative name, which was selected to recall the romantic memory of a series of successful sports racing cars of the late 1950s and early 1960s. First, though, a point of detail: whereas the older car was always a Testa Rossa (two words), the modern car is a Testarossa (one word). I have found no reason for this, other than the fact that the name rolls off the tongue in one lovely musical gracenote.

Testa Rossa translates as 'red head'. a title derived from the crackle-finish red paint applied to the engine's cam covers. In fact, the 1950s Testa Rossas weren't the first to have this paint finish, but somehow the name stuck.

Although the first Testa Rossa arrived in 1956 as a development of the 2-litre four-cylinder 500 Mondial sports racer, the name is always associated with the highly successful series of sports racers which first appeared in 1958 to meet new regulations imposed by the *Commission Sportive Internationale* (CSI), the governing body of motor sport.

Unlike its 'second division' position nowadays, the World Sports Car Championship equalled the World Formula 1 Championship in importance during the 1950s. One of the greatest years was 1957, when four manufacturers – Ferrari, Maserati, Jaguar and Aston Martin – contested the championship with increasingly powerful, big-engined cars. Throughout its history, motor racing progress has been punctuated by fears about cars becoming *too* powerful, and 1957 was such a year. Ferrari and Maserati were squeezing close to 400bhp from their 4.1-litre and 4.5-litre engines, and the CSI's reaction to their power struggle was to impose a new 3-litre limit for 1958 and beyond. This was why the Testa Rossa was born.

As usual, Maranello, with its bewildering range of engine permutations, was well placed to meet the new requirements. At the same time, it could kill two birds with one stone by offering the same car to American customers, who were also given a 3-litre class that year by the Sports Car Club of America (SCCA). Ferrari's sports racers had always been rugged, powerful cars, but for customer use they also needed to be relatively simple.

So it was that Ferrari's design team, led by *Ingegnere* Andrea Fraschetti, rejected two complex four-cam solutions – the existing Lampredi V12 used in the 315S and 335S sports racing cars and the Dino four-cam V6 being developed in Formula 1 – in favour of further development of the Colombo 250GT 3-litre V12.

With foreknowledge of the regulation changes, Fraschetti began producing what could be described as a prototype Testa Rossa early in 1957, and this hybrid car – yet to be known as a Testa Rossa – made its race debut at the Nürburgring 1000Kms in May. It used an existing chassis design (with 92.5in. wheelbase and De Dion rear suspension) of the type normally powered by 3.8-litre and 4-litre four-cam V12 engines, but into this frame was fitted the two-cam 250GT 3-litre V12.

The experienced Belgian driver Olivier

Gendebien set a promising sixth fastest practice time, but was transferred to a works 335S for the race after Wolfgang von Trips suffered an accident during practice when he got his brake and accelerator pedals mixed up. Ferrari team manager Romolo Tavoni needed a replacement driver urgently for the 'prototype Testa Rossa', and recruited a virtual unknown, Carlo Marolli, on the spot to partner American Masten Gregory in the car. Gregory fought the new car up to fourth place against bigger-engined opposition in the early stages, but then had to watch as the tardy Marolli slipped back to tenth place.

A second 3-litre prototype was readied for Le Mans in June, this car having a larger 500 Testa Rossa chassis (from the old four-cylinder car bearing the name) with live axle rear suspension. Its body was quite different, Sergio Scaglietti's design (as shown in the immaculate example above) introducing a shape which would become a Testa Rossa hallmark – the 'pontoon' body. The nickname was prompted by the car's unusual frontal styling, wherein its wings were virtually separated from the nose, almost like a catamaran, to allow plenty of air to cool the front brake. The pontoon body was later discarded because of poor aerodynamics.

DEVELOPING PROTOTYPES
Competitive despite smaller engine

The original Nürburgring prototype damaged a piston in its enlarged 3. 1-litre two-cam V12 before Le Mans practice, but the new prototype fared well in the hands of Gendebien and Maurice Trintignant. Running, once again, in opposition to cars with much larger engines, this pair lay in second place until retiring with another burned piston.

Both Testa Rossa prototypes ran in August's Swedish Grand Prix at Rabelov, the Le Mans chassis now having its 3-litre V12 worked out in the definitive specification for 1958. Capacity stood at 2953cc from a 73mm bore and 58.8mm stroke, and power output was given as 300bhp at 7200rpm. Both cars,

driven by Gendebien/Trintignant and Gregory/ Wolfgang Seidel, retired in the early stages.

The final race of the 1957 World Sports Car Championship was held in November at Caracas, Venezuela, an unusual place for such a nail-biting showdown, for both Ferrari and Maserati were shooting for the title. Ferrari took its two Testa Rossa prototypes to back up its larger-engined cars in opposition to Maserati's brutal 450S machines. As it turned out, the contest rather fizzled out as Maserati suffered an incredible series of accidents which virtually destroyed its team of cars. Ferrari was left to win more or less as it pleased, and the two Testa Rossa prototypes came home third and fourth to help accumulate the points needed for the championship title. So ended a season which saw a rather special display of forward planning on Ferrari's part: its new Testa Rossa for the 1958 season was by now fully race-developed.

OFFICIAL LAUNCH
Works and customer cars

The Testa Rossa was launched officially at a press conference a fortnight after the return from Caracas, and two versions – works and customer specifications – were announced. While the works cars would use either live axle or De Dion rear suspension configurations, customer cars would all have the simpler live axle arrangement. Indeed, the first of nineteen customer cars built over that winter, one destined for John von Neumann, Ferrari's West Coast distributor in the USA, was displayed at the press conference.

The 3-litre two-cam V12's power output remained at the 300bhp set in Sweden, its final development the work of *Ingegnere* Carlo Chiti, who took over the role of chief engineer after Fraschetti was killed in a testing accident. The engine used conventional wet sump lubrication, and breathed through six twin-choke Weber carburettors. Apart from its tremendous power and fulsome spread of torque, this engine's great quality was its reliability, a vital factor in races which ran for between six and twenty-four hours.

The definitive Testa Rossa used the 'pontoon' bodywork which had appeared at Le Mans, and its chassis was a typically orthodox stout tubular frame. Transmission was by a four-speed gearbox mounted in line with the engine, damping was by old-fashioned lever arms, and braking continued to be by traditional finned drums (even though Jaguar had been using discs for seven years). It was a robust machine ideally suited to its task, but hardly state-of-the-art.

Ferrari's works Testa Rossas, backed up by a growing number of privateer cars, virtually swept the board in 1958, although it has to be said that their opposition was meagre. Maserati, licking its financial wounds, was temporarily retired from motor racing, Jaguar's D-types were long in the tooth and now run only by privateers, and Aston Martin was still developing its new 3-litre DBR1. Against these, Ferrari was tremendously well prepared for the 3-litre era. It would have been a disaster for its Testa Rossas to fail to win the 1958 World Sports Car Championship. But they won with ease, taking four of the five championship rounds in which they took part – the only exception was the Nürburgring 1000Kms, which the brilliant British driver Stirling Moss won for the second year running in an Aston Martin.

The season began at Buenos Aires in January with five Testa Rossas (three works, two private) on the grid, Phil Hill/Peter Collins winning from Mike Hawthorn/von Trips to give Ferrari the top two places. Another 1-2 victory came at Sebring in March with Hill/Collins in front again from Luigi Musso/Gendebien – this time there were three privateers to support the works trio. No privateers went to Sicily for the Targa Florio in May, but three of Ferrari's four works cars finished in first, third and fourth places – Musso/Gendebien from Hawthorn/von Trips and Hill/Collins.

FIRST AT LE MANS
A works car wins

Although Moss pipped the works Testa Rossa quartet at the Nürburgring in June, all four cars finished in second to fifth places, with Hawthorn/Collins leading home von Trips/Gendebien, Hill/Musso and Seidel/Gino Munaron. Three customer cars brought the total Testa Rossa entry to seven, but for Le Mans three weeks later ten would take part. Ferrari returned to top form for this fifth championship round, although poor reliability meant that only one of the four works cars, that of Hill/Gendebien, finished. Fortunately, the singleton was first!

It was a season of rare domination, for Testa Rossas took nine of the fifteen available top three positions in those five races. Their opposition was not the strongest ever, but the carefully developed Testa Rossas enabled Ferrari to win the World Sports Car Championship by the handsome margin of thirty-eight points to Aston Martin's sixteen. It was such a convincing display that Ferrari felt no need to attend the final championship round, the Tourist Trophy at Goodwood.

Development continued as the season progressed. First came the substitution of the

live axle and front-mounted four-speed gearbox with a De Dion rear end combined with a transaxle five-speed 'box intended to counter front weight bias. By the time of the Targa Florio, Ing. Chiti had also begun to institute new fully enclosed front bodywork as he suspected the 'pontoon' style of promoting aerodynamic lift and instability at speed. Modern telescopic shock absorbers replaced the old lever arms, and eventually Ferrari bowed to technology by fitting discs in place of drum brakes.

With the championship won by June, the rest of 1958 was spent on developing updated Testa Rossas for the 1959 season. Their new Pininfarina-designed bodywork was constructed by former Maserati body builder Medardo Fantuzzi, since he was short of work and Ferrari's normal sub-contractor, Scaglietti, was occupied with production manufacture.

A LEANER YEAR IN 1959
Title handed over to Aston Martin

Perhaps Ferrari rested a little too much on its laurels, with three consecutive championship titles behind it. The 1959 season opened at Sebring, and this was the only race Ferrari would win that year. Three Testa Rossas were entered, and two of them led. Dan Gurney/ Chuck Daigh were left in front after Hill/ Gendebien retired with differential failure, but the two star drivers took over the Gurney/ Daigh car to ensure that it stayed in front, Hill driving superbly through the rain. The

illustration above shows Frenchman Jean Behra in the second placed car at Sebring in 1959.

Three works Testa Rossas went to the Targa Florio, but all suffered further breakages with their new transaxle differentials. Gurney/ Cliff Allison and Jean Behra/Tony Brooks led, but even if the Ferraris had survived it is doubtful whether they could have kept at bay the nimble little 1.5-litre Porsches which were snapping at their heels. Thereafter, the Testa Rossas ceased to have the necessary reliability and Aston Martin won the last three championship rounds to take the title by twenty-four points to Ferrari's twenty-two.

Although Aston Martin had refined its DBR1 into a reliable and fast car, Ferrari's organisation had slightly fallen apart in 1959. The Testa Rossas were fast enough, but uncharacteristically fragile: as well as their differential failures, their Le Mans effort was spoiled by engine casting defects.

The Testa Rossas raced on into 1960, but now were joined more regularly by Dino V6-engined sports cars based on Ferrari's Formula 1 machinery. New rules meant that the Testa Rossa's elegant lines were rather spoiled by full-size windscreens and wipers.

Looking as if it was getting its act together once more, Ferrari won the first World Sports Car Championship race at Buenos Aires with Hill/Allison beating Richie Ginther/von Trips, but then came a lean spell. Private Testa Rossas were left to uphold Maranello honour at Sebring after the works trio was withdrawn

Trips/Ginther joined the second-placed Mairesse/Giancarlo Baghetti car after their 246SP's steering broke, and the Mexican Rodriguez brothers (Pedro and Ricardo) finished third. As if to ram home the message, there was even a private '60 specification Testa Rossa, driven by Hap Sharp/Hissom, in fourth place.

Only one Testa Rossa went to the Targa Florio alongside a pair of rear-engined 246SPs, but Pedro Rodriguez (sharing with his younger brother once more) retired it by running off the road, smashing its fuel tank too badly to continue – Ferrari scored another win with one of the 246SPs. A lone Testa Rossa for the Rodriguez duo went to the Nürburgring, and this time finished second behind a Birdcage Maserati.

LE MANS SWANSONG IN 1962
Beating the new generation
Since the Testa Rossas remained the powerhouses of the World Sports Car Championship, they looked on paper to be the cars for Le Mans. And so it turned out in this exciting race. The Rodriguez brothers' private Testa Rossa provided the fireworks, battling with the Hill/Gendebien and Mairesse/Mike Parkes works cars for twenty-two hours until suffering a broken piston. The works Testa Rossas survived to allow Hill/Gendebien to lead home a Ferrari 1-2, the pressure from the spectacular Mexicans having forced the winners to a record race average speed of 115.9mph.

This was one of the most convincing displays in the Testa Rossa's four-year reign at the top, and it clinched the World Sports Car Championship for Ferrari. There was no need to worry about the last round at Pescara, but all the same Ferrari entered one 246SP and lent a works Testa Rossa to the privateer Scuderia Centro Sud team for Lorenzo Bandini/Giorgio Scarlatti to drive. And, as if to give the Testa Rossa the perfect retirement present, the Bandini/Scarlatti partnership actually won.

As it turned out, the Testa Rossa was not quite consigned to history, for the following season, race organisers, fearing that the CSI's new GT classes would have less appeal for spectators, allowed so-called 'prototypes' with a maximum capacity of 4 litres to run. Ferrari developed a 4 litre V12 to 390bhp, and installed it in one experimental Testa Rossa (now designated 330TR/LM) for Le Mans, to be driven by those two old hands, Hill and Gendebien.

This race really was the conclusion of the Testa Rossa's front-line career, and it was a happy ending. The car won by forty-one miles to give the evolutionary Testa Rossa line its fourth Le Mans success in five years. It was also the third time that Hill and Gendebien had won together for Ferrari, and Gendebien's fourth victory in this classic event.

Looking back on the 'other' Testa Rossa's racing career three decades ago, it was as significant to sports racing car development as its modern namesake is to road car evolution. Indeed, with the perspective of time, it can be seen as probably the greatest sports racing Ferrari ever. It is fitting that its romantic name lives on today.

---

because of a dispute with the organisers – they insisted that a particular type of fuel should be used by all competitors, and Ferrari, with its commitment to Shell, refused to enter under these conditions.

Since the Targa Florio's twisty course suited agile cars, Ferrari entered only two Testa Rossas, now with independent rear suspension in place of the De Dion lay-out, alongside three of its smaller V6-engined sports racers. Both of the V12 cars were damaged during practice, one of them beyond repair. The patched-up survivor made the race for Ginther/Allison to drive, but Ginther crashed it.

There was a partial return to form for the two Testa Rossas entered at the Nürburgring for Hill/von Trips (with independent rear suspension) and Allison/Willy Mairesse (De Dion). The Hill/von Trips car suffered engine failure while leading, but Hill joined the other Testa Rossa for the closing stages of the race to help secure third place.

LE MANS – AGAIN
Pipping Porsche to the post
Once again Ferrari was badly placed in the championship, and needed to win at Le Mans to have any hope of taking the title. At least its rivals, Porsche and Maserati (back in the fray with its Birdcage car) were splitting the points which Ferrari was missing. Since brute horsepower and reliability formed the key to winning Le Mans, with its three-mile Mulsanne Straight, Ferrari concentrated on the Testa Rossas for this race, sending a team of five.

This weight of numbers was just as well, for two of the Testa Rossas ran out of fuel in the early stages owing to a mistake in consumption calculations. Two others, however, ran superbly to give Ferrari first and second places. Gendebien/Paul Frère remained in the lead from the second hour to the twenty-fourth, and Ricardo Rodriguez/André Pilette moved into second place during the fourteenth hour. This was enough to wrest the championship title from Porsche by thirty points to twenty-six, and to give the Testa Rossa its second crown in three years. But still there was life left in a design which dated back to 1957; never has a sports racing Ferrari enjoyed such a long life at the top of the racing tree.

SHARK-NOSE TESTA ROSSAS
The third championship title
The 1961 season really was to be the Testa Rossa's last, for a new GT-based championship (for closed coupé 'production' cars) was on the way for 1962. The Testa Rossas would indeed go out with a bang, winning three of the season's five races, although Ferrari was also developing and racing rear-engined Dino cars alongside them. Further updating work brought sleek new Fantuzzi bodies with the divided 'shark-nose' front radiator opening characteristic of all racing Ferraris that year.

Ferrari made a brilliant start to the new season at Sebring, with '61 specification Testa Rossas taking the top three places. The faithful pairing of Hill/Gendebien won, von

DESIGN AND DEVELOPMENT

Ferrari and Pininfarina produced the Testarossa by carefully revising every aspect of the Berlinetta Boxer's radical design

FOR TEN YEARS, the Berlinetta Boxer had been the supercar flagship of Ferrari's range. It had been steadily developed following its launch in 1971 as the 365GT4 BB in 4.4-litre form, becoming upgraded in 1976 to 512BB designation by having its engine bored out to nearly 5 litres, and finally gaining Bosch K-Jetronic fuel injection in 1982 to become the 512BBi.

By 1978, even though the Boxer still looked just about the most modern supercar in production, thoughts at Maranello began to turn to its replacement. Although it is undeniably true that further development would have allowed the Boxer, just like the Porsche 911, to live on for years and years, one must remember that Ferrari has never been a company to rest on its laurels. After all, Enzo Ferrari, in response to being asked which is his favourite among all the cars he has made, must have answered a thousand times, 'The one I build tomorrow.'

TESTAROSSA RATIONALE
Preparing for worldwide markets

Among the many targets for its new twelve-cylinder car, high on Ferrari's list was the need to re-enter the lucrative American market. Although its 'bread and butter' V8-engined cars could be sold in the USA, the Boxer had never been able to meet American safety and exhaust emissions regulations. So it was that Ferrari had gone through the 1970s unable to sell twelve-cylinder cars – the most profitable ones – in the USA.

This was no accident, for the USA's forthcoming crash test and pollution requirements were known by the world's car makers when the Boxer was being planned. Ferrari, however, was not terribly bothered about meeting American needs since there was every reason to believe that the supercar market in the USA would decline as a result. The company also felt that there was little point in spending a great deal of time and money suffocating the new flat-12's prodigious power output and slapping on huge crash-resistant bumpers; with his pursuit of supercar perfection, Enzo Ferrari was not interested in such compromises. The Boxer would be sold chiefly in Europe, and he was convinced that the market was big enough for the limited production that he had in mind. In this respect, therefore, the Testarossa marked a significant change in thinking.

The division of responsibility at Maranello for developing the Testarossa fell between three men: *Dottore Ingegnere* Angelo Bellei of the Project Department, *Ingegnere* Nicola Materazzi of the Engine Department and *Ingegnere* Maurizio Rossi of the Experimental Department. Although Ing. Bellei has since retired and Ing. Materazzi has left Ferrari, Ing. Rossi remains at Maranello and is now in charge of quality control. Ing. Rossi emphasises that the rationale behind the Testarossa was one of subtly refining the 512BB's qualities.

'There were many areas which we wanted to improve in developing the Boxer into the Testarossa,' he says. 'First of all, the new car had to have very beautiful lines, as it would be following on from a very attractive car. Perhaps the Boxer's worst defect was its lack of practicality. Although there was plenty of room inside for two people, there was very little space for their luggage – just a tiny area in the nose, and almost nothing inside the car. It was a superb machine to drive, but not very useful for a touring holiday.

'We also decided quite early on that the water radiators should be moved from the front to the sides of the car, as on single-seater and sports racing cars. Not only would this allow much more

Ingegnere Maurizio Rossi, *above*, of the Experimental Department at Maranello was an important figure in the design of the Testarossa. The car's shape was born at Pininfarina's impressive *Studi e Ricerche* centre, *right*, at Cambiano, outside Turin

luggage room in the front, but it would also concentrate more mass in the centre of the car, improving driveability and handling. It is particularly undesirable to have mass at a car's extremes as this creates a higher polar moment of inertia, which can make handling unpredictable near the limit.

'There were several other benefits in putting the radiators at the sides of the car. Improved aerodynamics was one, since we no longer needed radiator apertures directly in the airstream at the front. This change also enabled us to have a simpler hose system between radiators and engine, without the pipes passing through the cockpit.

'Side-mounted radiators, of course, made the car wider, but this conveniently allowed us to use the wider tyres which we felt were necessary to improve traction and grip. The Boxer's relative lack of traction at the rear was one of its weaknesses, as its rear tyres were only marginally wider than the front ones. Since we were planning a significant increase in power output for the Testarossa, we knew that larger rear tyres would be essential.'

PININFARINA'S ROLE
Working partnership

In reply to the question asking whether the Testarossa was conceived by Pininfarina or Ferrari, Rossi answered, in a typically Italian response, with a metaphor.

'It's hard to say looking back on it. It's like asking which came first, the chicken or the egg. No, to be serious, Ferrari normally begins by giving Pininfarina a brief, defining the parameters of the new model we have in mind. We tell them the configuration of engine and chassis, the wheelbase and track, a minimum size for the passenger compartment, the luggage space, and so on. We try to give as full an idea as possible of the concept and character of the car.

'Rather than design cars ourselves at Maranello, we go to Pininfarina because, in our opinion, it is the best styling company at the moment. We have a long association going back many years, and an excellent working relationship.'

So it was that Pininfarina was commissioned in early 1978 to present its first design renderings for the new Testarossa. It is rare for Pininfarina to release details of designs from a car's gestation period, but on our visit we were shown a selection of the Testarossa ideas that did not make it. They are reproduced here.

A seven-strong design team led by Leonardo Fioravanti, General Manager of Pininfarina's *Studi e Ricerche* (Study & Research) centre at Cambiano, twenty miles east of Turin, produced its initial studies following faithfully Ferrari's brief on dimensions and configuration.

Initially a front radiator was to be retained. Early Testarossa proposals show a clear family resemblance to the Boxer and the 308GTB, both of which had been styled by Pininfarina. The front radiator grille, and small side intakes designed solely to feed air to the engine, can be seen clearly on these 1978 drawings.

By the time this first batch of designs had been produced, Ferrari's thinking had moved on to a side radiator layout. So it is that later design renderings show larger air intakes on the flanks for these radiators, and a gradual departure from the Boxer-derived shape. Some sketches show banana-shaped sill profiles between the wheels, as pioneered on Pininfarina's famous 'ideal aerodynamic' design exercise of 1978, but this shape was discarded because of its anticipated production cost. Two renderings also show separate rear aerofoils, but Ferrari felt this suggestion was an aesthetically unacceptable solution to the need to counter aerodynamic lift.

Ferrari's change to a side radiator brief, as well as Pininfarina's knowledge that it was working a long way ahead on a crucial new model, meant that more than three years passed between presentation of the first proposals and approval for the Testarossa's final design.

Once the concept for the final shape of the car had been accepted by Ferrari, the next step, late in 1981, was to construct a full-scale polystyrene model. Initially this was shaped to conform with the approved drawings, but further changes – some aesthetic, others practical – were made as the rough three-dimensional form was refined. Pininfarina prefers to model at full-scale as this gives a better idea of the finished lines, and polystyrene is used rather than clay because it is lighter and easier to work. When the final shape had been fixed, it was replicated in resin to provide a durable full-scale model.

Two areas of change can be seen clearly by comparing the 'definitive' rear three-quarter rendering with the final model: a sloping plexiglass rear window was discarded in favour of a flat engine cover to provide better heat extraction, and the NACA ducts on the car's flanks were replaced by finned – or straked – apertures to improve air flow to the radiators. Otherwise, the broad rear wheelarches and tail treatment shown in the rendering are identical to the finished form.

The full-scale resin model still exists, and it was wheeled out for us to photograph in the presentation hall where it was first seen by Enzo Ferrari and his senior management. This room, a perfectly lit arena the size of a badminton court, with a white marble floor, white walls and a plain ceiling, contains two remote-control circular platforms at its far end to enable clients to study from all angles the design which Pininfarina hopes they will accept.

From a distance this mock Testarossa appears just like the real thing, but closer observation shows subtle signs that this scarlet vision is merely an artificial shell. All the panel lines are indicated by fine black painted strips, there is a basic dummy interior behind the smoked glass, there are no outside mirrors, the production car's air conditioning intake in the front spoiler is missing, the badging details are different and the windscreen wiper design is slightly dissimilar.

As well as serving its purpose in gaining approval for the final design, this resin model also went to Pininfarina's wind tunnel at Grugliasco for aerodynamic evaluation. No significant design changes were made, although the Testarossa's Cd of 0.36 fell well short of the 0.30 benchmark which Audi was then achieving for its imminent 100 model. From the beginning, the large apertures leading to the side radiators were filled with five strakes to provide a form of grille, as regulations required – at first these strakes were black, but a body colour finish was quickly substituted.

While Pininfarina was working in the wind tunnel, Ferrari began to build its first prototype in the Experimental Department at Maranello, concentrating on developing its mechanical components. This was very much a test 'hack' without a fully-trimmed interior. With one built, a further fifteen were manufactured for Ferrari by ITCA, the Turin-based company which went on to build production Testarossa chassis and bodies. As with the production process, Pininfarina painted and trimmed these prototypes, so that by the time they were ready for testing they bore a close resemblance to the finished Testarossa.

ENGINE DEVELOPMENT
Improving the flat-12
At the time of the Testarossa's conception, the Berlinetta Boxer's flat-12 engine had plenty of development life left in it. It was born in 1971 at the same time as the Boxer, and indeed the car took this name from its engine – the horizontally-opposed piston motion can be likened to a punching action.

Dottore Ingegnere Giuliano de Angelis was responsible for designing this flat-12, and followed Ferrari racing practice in his thinking. A flat-12 is an unusual engine configuration, but Ferrari had developed three separate racing units of this layout in the five years before a roadgoing version was conceived. In 1964 a 1.5-litre flat-12 developing 220bhp at 11,500rpm had been designed by Ing. Mauro Forghieri for Formula 1, and it was honed into a superb unit by the time the regulations were altered to a 3-litre capacity limit at the end of 1965.

There was another 2-litre flat-12, giving 290bhp at 11,800rpm, in 1968 before Ing. Forghieri's definitive 3-litre flat-12, the Formula 1 312B engine, arrived in 1969. This would go on to propel Ferrari cars to thirty-seven Grand Prix victories between 1970 and 1979, its power output growing from 450bhp at 11,000rpm to 515bhp at 12,300rpm by the end of its competitive life.

This, therefore, was the route which led to the design of Dr Ing. de Angelis's roadgoing flat-12. The performance and reliability of this configuration had been proved by the Racing Department, and there were distinct practical advantages too – a flat-12 would be compact, it would allow good rearward vision for a mid-engined car, and it would lower the centre of gravity. Transverse mounting of the existing V12, as in the Lamborghini Miura, was considered early on, but a new flat-12 was the favoured solution from the beginning.

Its design closely followed that of the 312B engine, but its capacity, at 4.4 litres, was rather larger to achieve the necessary power and to make

use of some existing V12 components, like pistons and con rods. Many V12 design features – like twin overhead camshaft cylinder heads and an 8.8:1 compression ratio – were carried over, but one change was to use toothed rubber timing belts instead of chains in the interests of refinement, reliability and cheapness. Whereas the Daytona had drawn fuel through six twin-choke downdraught Weber carburettors, the flat-12 would use four triple-choke Webers.

Although it shared the V12's capacity, the flat-12 had a little more muscle: power went up from the Daytona's 352bhp at 7500rpm to 360bhp at 7000rpm (but 20bhp more was seen on some prototype engines). The torque figure of 311lb ft was slightly lower than the Daytona's 315lb ft, although the flat-12 peaked a useful 1000rpm lower down the rev range at 4500rpm.

POWER VERSUS EMISSIONS
A careful balancing act
Through the Boxer's 13-year lifespan, the flat-12 underwent two significant changes. In July 1976 came a 5-litre version with bore and stroke increased from 81 × 72mm to 82 × 78mm, and a higher compression ratio of 9.2:1. The need for this arose because of tougher European noise and pollution regulations – capacity had to increase just to preserve the Boxer's performance. Torque rose to 331lb ft at 4300rpm, but maximum power dropped to 340bhp at 6200rpm because the larger engine could not rev as high. The opportunity was also taken to give the engine a dry sump lubrication system to conquer oil surge problems under heavy braking and hard cornering. Then, in 1982, came the 512BBi with Bosch K-Jetronic mechanical fuel injection to replace the Weber carburettors.

Concurrent with the 512BBi being prepared for production, Ing. Materazzi's team was working on further improvements to the flat-12 for the Testarossa. Their work had two aims: to 'cleanse' the engine so that it could meet American emissions requirements, and to improve its torque characteristics. Although the flat-12 had always been formidably powerful, it lacked the flexible response which is so important for day-to-day driveability.

As other manufacturers were finding at the same time, Ferrari realised that the answer to improving many aspects of engine performance – power, flexibility, fuel consumption, efficiency – lay in using four valves per cylinder. However, this was not new technology at Maranello, for *quattrovalvole* heads, directly derived from racing experience, had already been developed for introduction on the 3-litre V8 engine in 1982.

It is worth dwelling on the theory of four-valve heads, as these were almost entirely responsible for the Testarossa's 50bhp gain over the 512BBi. To return to the carburettor flat-12 for a moment, in

Under Leonardo Fioravanti, a team of seven designers started work in 1978 on Pininfarina's styling proposals. These renderings are a small selection of those put to Ferrari.
The top two sketches in the first column are details of the finished design; the remainder are unsuccessful ideas. Initially the brief was for a front-mounted radiator, and the blue car follows this format with small side air intakes to the engine; later these intakes grow larger.
The bottom two renderings in the third column show the Testarossa outline beginning to emerge

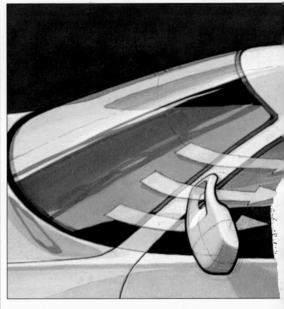

this form the engine had one carburettor choke and two valves per cylinder. The introduction of fuel into the cylinder relied on the depression caused by the piston moving downwards. As a performance engine, it had 'top-end' characteristics promoted by the valves having considerable overlap – the inlet and exhaust valves spent a relatively long time in the open position.

When you come to replace carburettors with injection, with a continuous spray of fuel, this overlap is undesirable in emissions terms since some of the fuel is squirted out through the exhaust. To meet emissions targets, therefore, the overlap period had to be shortened on two-valve fuel-injected engines, causing power reduction. The only way enough fuel/air mixture could be fed into the engine was by increasing the proportion of each combustion chamber occupied by valves – in other words, using four valves. By this means, the short overlap period needed for a clean exhaust could be retained without sacrificing performance. An added advantage is better power lower down the rev range.

'Four-valve technology means that the whole engine must be re-worked,' says Ing. Rossi. 'It is not sufficient just to add a couple of valves to each combustion chamber: attention also has to be directed to the length, volume and shape of the intake and exhaust manifolds. During bench testing of our experimental Testarossa engines, we worked very hard. You know, it was like playing around with an organ's pipes. We took many different lengths, shapes and sizes of intake and exhaust tubes, and we tried every combination until we arrived at the most satisfactory result. So, we put in a great deal of time in order to maximise power *and* to have the best torque at any point on the power curve.

'Apart from this, what we gained with four valves was a sufficiently low level of exhaust emissions to meet regulations throughout the world, plus lower fuel consumption. It had been impossible on the two-valve Boxer to meet US emissions regulations, but after a lot of work we obtained a Federal Emissions Certificate for the Testarossa.

'We changed the fuel injection to a Bosch KE-Jetronic injection system: K-Jetronic, which otherwise was used in all our models, is a continuous spray mechanical system with hydraulic regulation of the metering unit, whereas KE-Jetronic has electronic fuel regulation. The ignition system was unaltered, apart from introducing a computerised ignition programme. This constantly decides the best advance angle for power, fuel consumption and exhaust emissions.'

REFINING THE PACKAGE
From Boxer to Testarossa

As far as the rest of the mechanical specification is concerned, the evolution from Boxer to Testarossa consisted of refining the existing design, concentrating on three main areas – braking efficiency, ease of driving and noise insulation.

'Since we were planning to increase the car's performance,' continues Ing. Rossi, 'we also needed to improve the brakes. We introduced a completely new system with larger 12in. discs and calipers, so that there could be no shortcomings in any conditions – whether braking from very high speed or the kind of sustained use which can cause fade.

'Another aim was to make this top model in our range – I'm not counting the limited edition GTO – a much easier car to drive. While its performance had to be even better than the 512BB's, we also

This final design rendering, *above*, is close to the finished form, but there are distinct differences. A plexiglass panel forms the engine cover, the side strakes are missing and the lines are slightly more rounded. These features were modified on a full-scale model

The finished model was duplicated in resin, *left*, for Ferrari's approval and wind tunnel evaluation. It looks like a real car, but panel lines are painted on, door mirror is missing and air conditioning intake has yet to appear

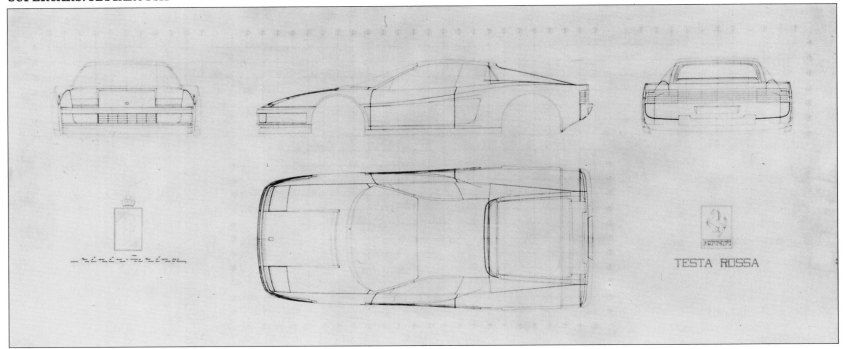

Pininfarina's blueprint for the Testarossa's body outline, *top*. The plan view shows clearly how the body broadens to the rear where intakes taper in. A finished car in 1988 specification, *above*, pictured in front of Fiorano's control centre; Longines/Olivetti timing equipment helped in assessing development changes

wanted it to be easy for anyone to drive, and capable of covering great distances without making the driver tired. This was all part of our concept of making the Testarossa a true Grand Touring car.

'So it was that we gave the Testarossa a high standard of interior comfort, light controls and a good ride, while taking care that none of these things would sacrifice any of its sporting appeal. One of the big complaints about the 512BB was the weight of its clutch – it was both heavy and sharp. We discarded the old 8½in. double-plate clutch, replacing it with a 9½in. unit, and also refined the hydraulic actuation to reduce pedal weight. The result is a lighter, stronger and more reliable clutch.

'We worked to reduce internal noise and exhaust noise, the latter being something which impending regulations were to require in any case. Many mid-engined cars are very noisy, so we are proud of how quiet the Testarossa is – quite a lot of work went into insulating the engine and reducing vibration.

'Much work was also put into the chassis and body to reduce the car's overall weight while at the same time improving strength. The American market again dictated our target, since federal crash tests for front, rear and side impact had to be met by the Testarossa.

'With this concept of a comfortable high-performance car, it was necessary to have a good air conditioning system. This is particularly important in America, where a car without air conditioning is considered incomplete. We developed an automatic system with two possibilities: while you can regulate temperature and fan speed in the normal way, you can also give the driver and passenger different conditions.'

DEVELOPMENT TESTING
Looking for problems
After all the activity in the Experimental Department, the test programme got underway during 1982, starting with a thorough check of the first prototype's mechanical systems to ensure that

FIORANO
Ferrari's high-tech track

Other car manufacturers, like Porsche with Weissach and Alfa Romeo with Balocco, have test tracks, but few as small as Ferrari have this luxury. On top of this, Ferrari's Fiorano test track is so close to the factory that from the reception area you can hear the wailing of Grand Prix engines when the Racing Department is out testing. You can even see cars in action from the main road through Maranello – scoop shots of new Ferraris are usually two a penny . . .

Making the half-mile journey from the factory to the track is a sightseeing trip in itself. You drive straight out of the main gates down *Viale Dino Ferrari*, turn into *Via Gilles Villeneuve* and at the end of this rough road see a sign announcing *La Pista di Fiorano*. Here, behind barbed wire fences, is a testing facility as modern as can be found anywhere.

The layout of the 1.86 mile track is a figure of eight, designed in 1972 to incorporate characteristics of many of the world's great racing circuits. So it is that there are two hairpins (one to the right, the other to the left) mimicking those at Monaco, fast Monza and Silverstone bends, and, over the bridge, two sloping curves and a crest reminiscent of the once-great Nürburgring.

There are fourteen curves with radii varying between 15 and 404 yards, and the track's minimum width is 27.6ft. Modern Grand Prix Ferraris can lap the circuit in just over a minute, averaging over 105mph. My few laps in a Testarossa driven by Giorgio Enrico were some 35sec off that pace, but good enough to get the feel of the circuit.

What makes Fiorano so special is its system of Longines/Olivetti electronic timing equipment and closed-circuit television. There are forty-four sensors sprouting from the ground around the track like airport landing lights, and these are sited at roughly 50 yard intervals on the bends. By timing a car's progress on every part of the circuit, they are invaluable in adding objective evidence to a test driver's subjective assessment of suspension, braking, transmission and engine modifications. During the course of a lap, a car breaks the timing beam at each of these points, and a computer in the control room simultaneously prints out each of the elapsed times.

On top of all this, there are fourteen video cameras (one for each corner) so that a car's behaviour can be studied from the bank of monitors in the control room. This system gives engineers extra insight into how cars handle close to their limits.

While Fiorano was designed primarily for the Racing Department, it is used extensively in the development of every new production Ferrari. The information it can provide complements perfectly the knowledge gained during testing on public roads.

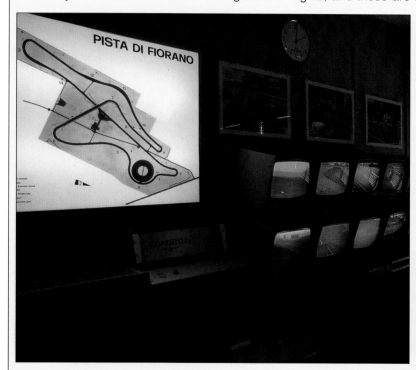

there was no potential for breakages or failures that might put the test drivers in danger. Special attention was paid to braking efficiency on a rolling road before any cars ventured out of the factory, first to Fiorano, then on public roads.

'The first prototype was ready to go on the track,' remembers Ing. Rossi, 'during the summer, which is a good time for testing because more problems are likely to occur when the weather is hot. Fiorano is a very severe test of a car, and after its first run we checked everything – suspension, brakes, tyres, engine temperatures. Whenever we encountered problems, of course, we had to make modifications.

'I remember that our main problem was in keeping the engine cool enough on a hot day. We had expected this possibility, since we had made the radical step of moving the radiators away from the car's nose. Fortunately the solution was quite simple – we had to increase the size of the apertures leading to the radiators to allow more air through, and work on the size and shape of the engine cover to make sure that hot air could be extracted efficiently.

'We also used test equipment at Fiorano to measure g-forces through the variety of turns there, and to analyse body vibrations. With some work on body resonances we were able to build in more refinement. Refining the exhaust system took a lot of time. We needed to have a relatively subdued exhaust note, but didn't want to sacrifice performance to achieve it. We tried many

The Testarossa resin model, *below*, and the production car, *right*, in the wind tunnel. Gradually peeling off the masking tape allowed the aerodynamic effect of each air intake to be measured. Further tests confirmed the car's basic stability

combinations of exhaust pipe length and section, as well as different silencer boxes, before we arrived at the production specification.'

Giorgio Enrico, the Chief Test Driver who has been with Ferrari for twenty-eight years, was responsible for the development testing. Enrico does not at once fit one's image of a flamboyant test driver, but he is highly regarded by his colleagues at Maranello. During his time there he has tested all Ferrari's road car designs as well as many of the racing machines, but he has never competed himself – 'I prefer to drive on my own.'

Part of Enrico's work has always involved analysing Ferrari's competition, so he has driven all the great supercars of the last three decades. Those he respects the most are the Lamborghini Countach and the Porsche 911 Turbo. However, like all other senior Ferrari personnel, he drives a very modest road car of his own – a Fiat Panda . . .

Most of the development was carried out over a period of two years with disguised prototypes pounding over roads in the region of Maranello. A standard route encompassing a wide variety of conditions was selected. Enrico and his team would head through the Appennine mountains to La Spezia on the Ligurian coast, and then return to Maranello on the *autostrada* via Parma and Modena. Enrico himself covered around 30,000 miles in six 'endurance' prototypes, helped by three other drivers.

HIGH-SPEED EVALUATION
Testing at Fiorano and Nardo

With so much of the engine development achieved in bench testing, much of the effort on the road was put into refining handling, roadholding and ride. Many permutations of spring and shock absorber rates were tried in order to exceed the Boxer's handling abilities *and* to improve ride quality.

A great deal of work was also put into the

brakes. The first Testarossa prototype began with 512BB discs carrying larger calipers, but very soon it became apparent that larger discs were necessary, with wider ducts in the nose to bring cool air to them. In keeping with the lightness of the other controls, the servo-assistance was uprated to reduce pedal pressure.

Anti-lock brakes (ABS) were never considered for the Testarossa – Ferrari has often been initially suspicious of new technological developments, and ABS is one. Many people at Maranello felt that ABS would be inappropriate for such an out-and-out driving machine as the Testarossa, but two other models – the 412i and the Mondial – have subsequently acquired such systems (by Bosch and Teves respectively) in order to test customer reaction and reliability. As this was being written, Ing. Rossi confirmed that ABS was being studied for the Testarossa – 'we go step by step'.

Considerable testing of the air conditioning system was necessary to ensure that it worked as well around town as at high speed. Crucial to this compromise was arriving at the right dimensions and position for an air inlet in the black bib spoiler under the front bumper. Rossi confesses that his team was reluctant to disturb the smooth nose profile with an intake duct for – of all things on a sporting car! – the air conditioning system, but this was the only position which worked effectively. If you examine the photographs of Pininfarina's resin model, you can see that originally there was no aperture.

High-speed evaluation was carried out at Nardo, a test track near the coast at Brindisi in southern Italy. Many manufacturers use Nardo, since its great advantage over other test bowls lies in having an eight-mile circular track. This is long enough to provide a very gently banked curvature, making it a safe place to reach 180mph or so in a road car. Shorter test tracks, like MIRA or Millbrook in

England, have such steeply banked turns that sustained speeds over 140mph become truly nail-biting.

Although Pininfarina's wind tunnel experiments had proved the Testarossa's basic aerodynamic stability, Ferrari engineers worked hard with subtly different front spoilers and rear bodywork angles to produce a good compromise between maximum speed and stability. The slightly rising lip at the tail of the finished car differs from the flat profile of the original full-scale model.

Tiny details required attention, too – the windscreen wipers are an example. Many supercars from small manufacturers show their lack of development in little ways, like having windscreen wipers which lift from the glass at high speed. Ferrari used wet days at Nardo to make sure that the Testarossa's pair of wipers (the Boxer had a single pantograph wiper) remained efficient at all speeds.

Winds coming off the sea often disrupted the high-speed runs, but eventually 295kmh (183.3mph) was obtained as a definitive top speed after much experimentation with body details. The top speed of production models would be quoted at 290kmh (180.2mph).

The conclusion of the development programme was crash testing for Type Approval. The cars which covered all those test miles, as well as two relatively unused prototypes, were shunted into concrete barriers and subjected to side impacts. Of those which escaped this ignominious end, all but three were destroyed, literally broken up and scrapped, because they were deemed unsuitable for sale to the public. The survivors were preserved by the Experimental Department for further development.

This destruction of prototypes is normal Ferrari practice. While other manufacturers often keep their prototypes, there has always been an indifference to posterity at Maranello. Just occasionally, Ferrari will sell a prototype if its quality matches production standards, but this was not the case with the Testarossa.

POST-LAUNCH EVOLUTION
Few modifications since 1984

It is a fine tribute to the soundness of the Testarossa's original design that very few changes have been made since production began after the car's public debut at the 1984 Paris Salon. Maranello people present at the show say that no other Ferrari since the Daytona has met with such public acclaim.

Lowering the driving mirror to a more aesthetically pleasing position, and fitting a matching mirror on the passenger side, has been the only important visual modification since 1984. This ungainly stalk of a rear-view mirror, mounted halfway up the windscreen pillar on the driver's side, was one of the Testarossa's most controversial aesthetic aspects when it was launched. Ing. Rossi explains that it was not much liked at Ferrari either, but that there was no alternative.

'At that time, EEC regulations required that the external mirror should give 100 per cent vision to the rear. With the Testarossa's broad rear wheelarches, it was possible to provide a complete view behind the car only by mounting the mirror in a relatively high position. We used only one mirror because a second one in the corresponding position on the passenger side would have been at almost 90° to the driver's line of vision – in other words, in an impossible place. The regulations changed in

1985 to accept that a proportion of the mirror's view could be obscured by the body, and this allowed us to mount mirrors on both sides in lower positions.'

Look hard at a current Testarossa and you might notice that it has five bolt attachments for its alloy wheels, whereas pre-1988 models had a single octagonal nut hub fixing. This change was simply for practicality, since the old design made it difficult for an owner to detach the wheel in the event of a puncture; despite the tool kit having a lead hammer with which to bash the hub spanner, it was beyond the strength of many owners to loosen the wheel. Once the puncture was repaired, the owner then had to return to his dealer to have the new wheel properly tightened, with a massive torque wrench, to 325lb ft.

Although the suspension geometry has not changed, the manufacturing method for the suspension members has. Whereas the Testarossa started out with with tubular steel wishbones, since late 1987 these pieces have been formed from pressed steel top and bottom halves welded together.

Apart from this, the only sub-surface changes have occurred where outside components have not met Ferrari's rigorous quality checks. In addition, Ferrari and Pininfarina continue to work together to improve quality of manufacture still further.

Enthusiasts who remember how fragile and corrosion-prone Ferraris once were always laugh when they hear talk of Ferrari and quality in the same breath, but vast progress has undeniably been made in the last ten years to approach Porsche and Mercedes-Benz standards. All the work that went into designing the Testarossa would be pointless if the cars were not going to last . . .

TESTAROSSA DISSECTED

Admirable engineering quality, purity of purpose — a closer look at one of the world's most desirable cars

EW SUPERCARS have a specification as formidable as the Testarossa's. While it is not as technologically avant-garde as, say, the Porsche 959, or even some far lesser German and Japanese products, it has admirable engineering quality and purity of purpose. These alone make it one of the world's most desirable cars.

The Testarossa has been criticised for lacking such state-of-the-art features as four-wheel drive and anti-lock braking, but Ferrari's history has been characterised by continual evolution rather than dramatic revolution. In carefully refining the Boxer's basic design, Ferrari has stood by this rationale to produce a masterpiece – albeit a somewhat conventional one – of performance engineering. So, what makes the Testarossa tick?

ENGINE
One of the world's finest

The Testarossa has one of the finest engines the world has ever seen – an aluminium alloy four-valve flat-12 (type designation F113A) mounted longitudinally behind the passenger compartment. Compared with the two-valve unit which preceded it in the Boxer, weight has been pared by 44lb (20kg). Its 82mm bore and 78mm stroke give a displacement of 4942cc, and the compression ratio is 9.3:1.

Peak power of 390bhp occurs at 6300rpm (although the engine will rev safely to 6800rpm), and the maximum torque of 361.6lb ft is developed at 4500rpm. Compared with the 512BBi, these figures are higher by 50bhp and 29lb ft. In terms of power relative to capacity, the Testarossa's 78.9bhp per litre compares with the 512BBi's 68.8bhp per litre. The graph on page 38 shows the smooth progression of the flat-12's power delivery – 193bhp is produced at 3000rpm, 276bhp at 4000rpm and 358bhp at 5000rpm.

The crankcase, cylinder block and cylinder heads are cast in aluminium/silicon alloy (Silumin), a lustrous metal which combines lightness with strength, as well as giving the engine a rare visual beauty. Cylinder liners are made of aluminium, their inner surfaces treated to a special hardening process with nickel and silicon (Nickasil) to promote longevity – they are shrink-fitted by reducing their temperature to −20°C.

Machined in Ferrari's traditional way from a single billet of hardened and tempered steel, with working surfaces nitrided for hardness, the crankshaft is a beautiful piece of work. Between the seven main bearings, con rods are connected up in pairs on each crankshaft throw, and run in thinwall bearings. Pistons are made in aluminium by Mahle, and carry two compression rings and one oil control ring. The cylinder firing order, shown in the diagram below, is 1-9-5-12-3-8-6-10-2-7-4-11.

The two cylinder heads are also made of silumin, and let into each of them are six domed combustion chambers shaped like rectangles with curved shorter ends. There are two exhaust and two inlet steel valves per cylinder, and a 12mm Champion

A6G spark plug sits in the centre of them. Valve seats are made of cast iron, and valve guides are in bronze. The inlet valves are inclined at 20° to the cylinder axis, and the exhaust valves at 21°. Valve timing is as follows: inlets open 12° before top dead centre (BTDC) and close 52° after bottom dead centre (ABDC); exhausts open 54° before bottom dead centre (BBDC) and close 10° after top dead centre (ATDC).

Concealed behind those gorgeous red crackle-finish cam covers are four overhead camshafts – one inlet and exhaust camshaft per bank – made of nitrided steel. These operate the valves through thimble-type tappets actuating steel valve springs. The required valve clearance is 0.20–0.25mm for inlets and 0.35–0.40mm for exhausts, the correct spacing being achieved by fitting circular shims into the tappets. The shims Ferrari uses vary in thickness from 3.25mm to 4.60mm in steps of 0.05mm, and have hardened surfaces.

Unlike Ferrari's earlier V12 engines, the camshafts are driven by a pair of toothed rubber Goodyear Supertorque PD belts connected directly to the crankshaft by two pulleys. These belts are longer than those of the 512BB, which used gear-driven pulleys mounted nearer the cylinder heads: their involute teeth (with a slightly rounded profile) give more precise location than the square teeth of the 512BB's belt. Timing belt tension is maintained by an idler wheel on each side.

Lubrication is by a dry sump system with two pumps, both geared from the inlet camshaft on the left-hand side as you look from the front. The scavenge pump draws hot oil from the sump and sends it first through the oil radiator (helped in its work by two electric fans) and then to the oil tank. A pressure pump brings oil back from the tank and through a filter to lubricate the moving parts. Total oil capacity is 27 pints (15.5 litres), and oil pressure holds 64psi at idle and between 71 and 85psi at 6000rpm.

There is also a crankcase emission control system to deal with oil vapours. Those from the crankcase are burned with the fuel, but vapour from the heads is drawn to the oil tank and returned to the lubrication system after it has condensed.

SIDE RADIATORS
A Testarossa innovation

Two large horizontal-flow Puma-Chausson water radiators are sited behind the car's side air intakes. Each radiator has an electric fan: a thermostat signals these fans to run when coolant temperature exceeds 84°C, and to switch off below 75°. Driven by a centrifugal pump turned by a chain from the crankshaft nose, this is a conventional closed-circuit cooling system using an expansion tank (fitted with a pressure-release valve) to compensate for the coolant's increased volume as it is heated. The water/antifreeze mixture is pressurised at 12.8psi.

A Magneti Marelli Microplex MED 120B electronic system controls ignition, varying the spark advance according to messages from sensors measuring engine speed, intake manifold vacuum and throttle position. There are two distributors, mounted on the aft end of each inlet camshaft, and two high-voltage coils. A socket for connection to a diagnostic tester (for tracing misfires and checking advance curve) is mounted on the left-hand side of the engine compartment near the ignition module. An AC Delco alternator sits ahead of the right-hand intake manifold, and is driven by a rubber belt from a pulley at the crankshaft's nose. The starter motor, a Bosch

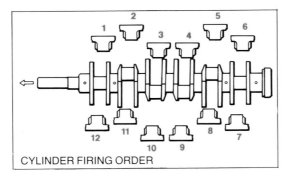

CYLINDER FIRING ORDER

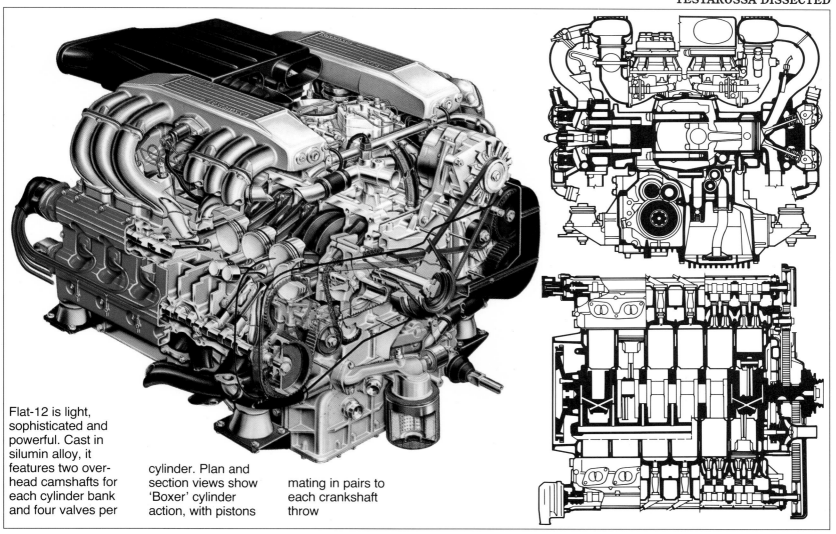

Flat-12 is light, sophisticated and powerful. Cast in silumin alloy, it features two overhead camshafts for each cylinder bank and four valves per cylinder. Plan and section views show 'Boxer' cylinder action, with pistons mating in pairs to each crankshaft throw

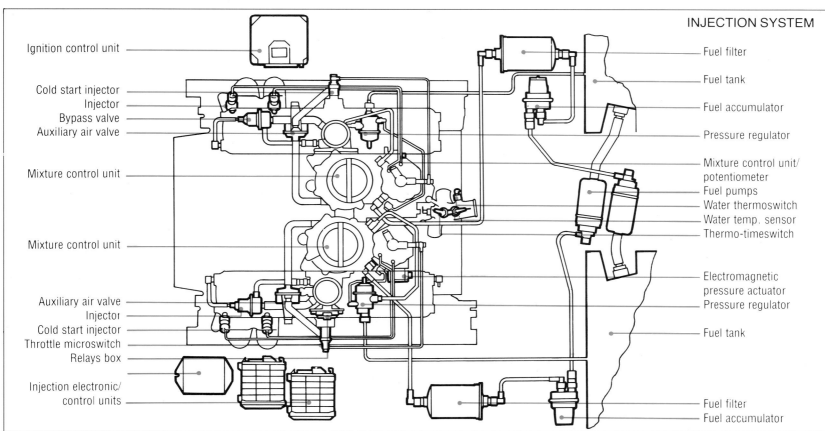

INJECTION SYSTEM

Ignition control unit

Cold start injector
Injector
Bypass valve
Auxiliary air valve

Mixture control unit

Mixture control unit

Auxiliary air valve
Injector
Cold start injector
Throttle microswitch
Relays box

Injection electronic/
control units

Fuel filter

Fuel tank

Fuel accumulator

Pressure regulator

Mixture control unit/
potentiometer
Fuel pumps
Water thermoswitch
Water temp. sensor
Thermo-timeswitch

Electromagnetic
pressure actuator
Pressure regulator

Fuel tank

Fuel filter
Fuel accumulator

component, sits beneath the crankcase.

Two individual Bosch KE-Jetronic systems, one per bank, provide the fuel injection. Fuel is drawn from the two fuel tanks – stretching well across the car's width for space and weight balance considerations – by a pair of Bosch electric pumps located between them. Total capacity of the tanks, tucked between engine and firewall, is 25.3 gallons (115 litres) plus a 3.9 gallon (18 litres) reserve.

There is a fuel accumulator for each system, and fuel then passes through nylon/paper filters to two mixture control units positioned above the crankcase. Twelve injectors supply a fine spray of fuel to the intake manifolds at a rate dependent on throttle opening and engine speed. The extra demands of cold starting are satisfied by two electromagnetic injectors to enrich the mixture, and an auxiliary air valve to allow a larger volume of the fuel/air mixture to the engine.

The exhaust system has two steel silencers and two smaller ones made of stainless steel.

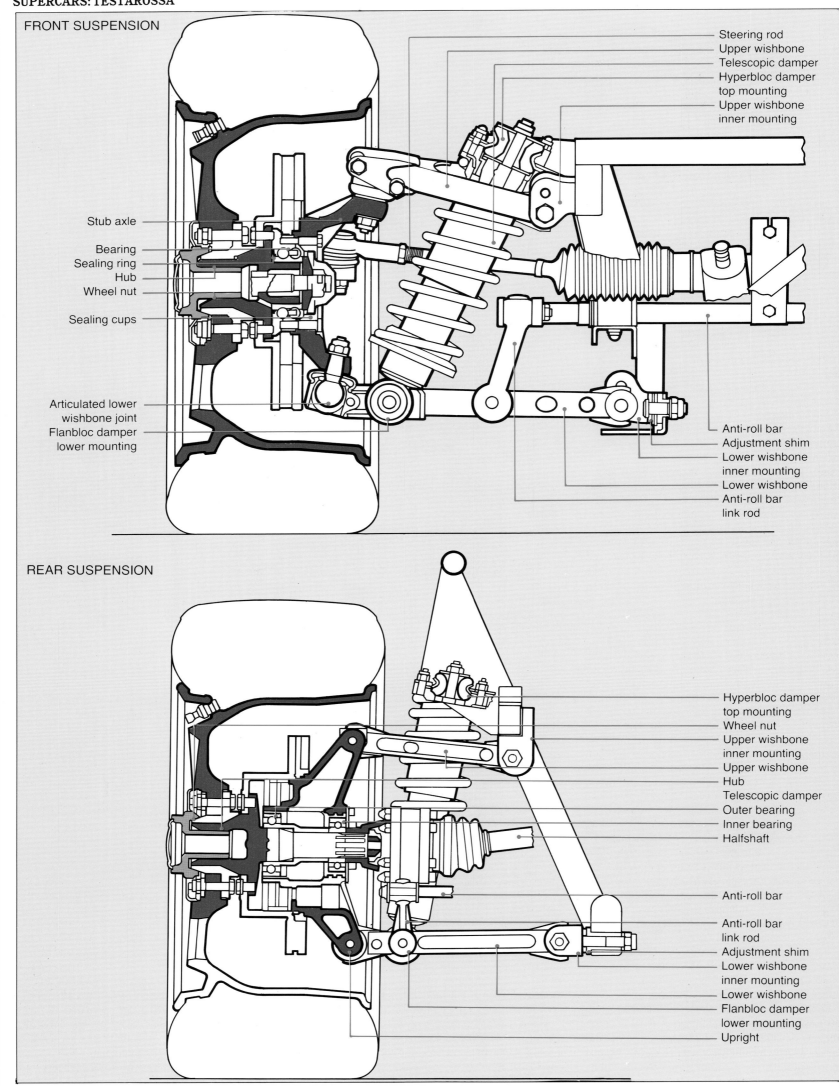

FRONT SUSPENSION

Steering rod
Upper wishbone
Telescopic damper
Hyperbloc damper
top mounting
Upper wishbone
inner mounting

Stub axle

Bearing
Sealing ring
Hub
Wheel nut

Sealing cups

Articulated lower
wishbone joint
Flanbloc damper
lower mounting

Anti-roll bar
Adjustment shim
Lower wishbone
inner mounting
Lower wishbone
Anti-roll bar
link rod

REAR SUSPENSION

Hyperbloc damper
top mounting
Wheel nut
Upper wishbone
inner mounting
Upper wishbone
Hub
Telescopic damper
Outer bearing
Inner bearing
Halfshaft

Anti-roll bar

Anti-roll bar
link rod
Adjustment shim
Lower wishbone
inner mounting
Lower wishbone
Flanbloc damper
lower mounting
Upright

TRANSMISSION
Compact arrangement

The Testarossa's Ferrari-manufactured five-speed gearbox sits beneath the engine in unit with a ZF limited slip differential, this neat assembly being contained within a single silumin casing almost as long as the engine itself.

Drive passes direct from the crankshaft via a flywheel to a Borg & Beck 9½in. double-plate dry clutch. This has one rigid plate and one plate with a spring hub, backed by a diaphragm pressure plate assembly. The clutch release is hydraulic with an overcentre helper spring, and is self-adjusting. From the clutch, gears step the drive downwards to a main shaft which passes across the differential to the gear cluster forward of it in the casing. This means, of course, that the gearbox is ahead of the rear axle line, and the clutch and flywheel behind it. There is a rod linkage to the gearlever.

This is a compact transmission arrangement, although it does have the disadvantage of placing the engine's mass relatively high in the car – the crankshaft is nearly 2ft above the ground. The alternative would have been a competition arrangement with gearbox and differential in line behind the engine (as on the limited-edition GTO), but the length of such an assembly would have encroached too much on cabin space to be practical for a Grand Touring car.

All five forward speeds have synchromesh, and ratios are 3.139, 2.014, 1.526, 1.167 and 0.875:1 – reverse is geared at 2.532:1. These give road speeds per 1000rpm of, respectively, 7.4mph (11.9kmh), 11.5mph (18.5kmh), 15.2mph (24.5kmh), 19.8mph (31.9kmh) and 26.5mph (42.6kmh).

Power is transmitted to the rear wheels by single-piece driveshafts, each shaft having at each end a constant velocity universal joint protected by a rubber boot. Oil capacity for the whole transmission assembly is 17 pints (9.5 litres); oil is circulated by a gear pump located on the front of the casing and operated by the input shaft.

SUSPENSION
Beefy independence

The Testarossa's suspension is independent all round, and sufficiently beefy to cope with the high cornering forces which the car can generate.

At the front are a pair of tubular steel wishbones mounted with their wider ends connecting to the chassis. The top wishbone tapers to a single mounting point at the top of the cast alloy upright, and extends inboard at an inclined angle, with the front attachment point higher than the rear, to give anti-dive characteristics under braking. The lower wishbone is larger, its two arms being linked by a pair of slender strengthening tubes. An angled coil spring enclosing a Koni 82P 2279 telescopic shock absorber connects from the bottom of the upright to a point on the chassis between the arms of the top wishbone. The anti-roll bar is connected by a short link rod to the rearward arm of the lower wishbone. Kingpin offset is minimised to reduce steering kickback and improve braking stability.

Rear suspension is similar in principle, but more substantial in order to handle the Testarossa's unusually large rear weight bias – front/rear weight distribution is 41.3/58.7 per cent. The most significant, and unusual, feature is *two* vertical coil springs and Koni 82P 2142 telescopic shock absorbers on each side, picking up at their bases from each arm of the lower wishbone and butting up against a broad longitudinal chassis beam at the top.

Carried over from the Boxer, these paired spring/

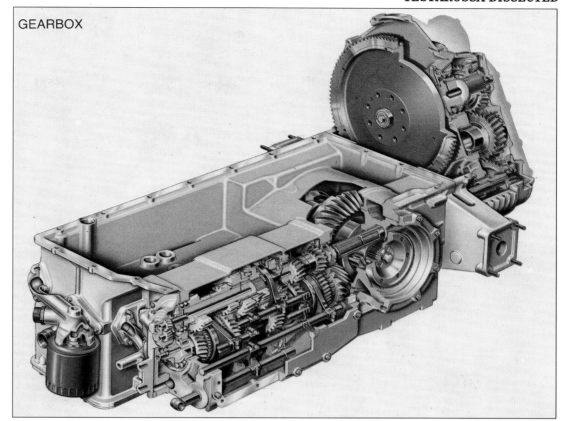

GEARBOX

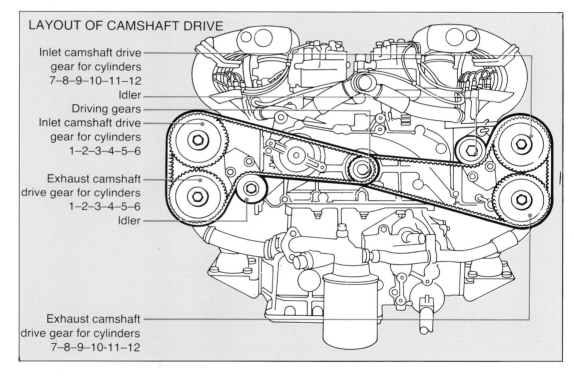

LAYOUT OF CAMSHAFT DRIVE

Inlet camshaft drive gear for cylinders 7–8–9–10–11–12
Idler
Driving gears
Inlet camshaft drive gear for cylinders 1–2–3–4–5–6

Exhaust camshaft drive gear for cylinders 1–2–3–4–5–6
Idler

Exhaust camshaft drive gear for cylinders 7–8–9–10–11–12

damper units are necessary to produce reliable damping characteristics. When shock absorbers have to work hard during fast cornering or over rough surfaces, they can fade as their oil heats up and loses viscosity. Sharing the load, two dampers provide more resistance to overheating, and also give firmer location for the lower wishbone.

The wishbones themselves – tubular steel on early cars, two sections of welded pressed steel on later ones – are both triangulated for extra strength, and have two mountings on the wheel uprights (there is only one on the front wishbones). An anti-roll bar connects with the lower wishbone via a short link rod picking up at the same point as the rear spring/damper unit.

Flexible Flanbloc rubber bushes provide cushioning where the wishbones mount to the chassis. The Koni shock absorbers have rubber bushes at the top to act as bump stops, and internal elastic bushes at the bottom for the rebound stops.

Hub rotation at front and rear is provided by double rows of ball bearings.

STEERING
Power assistance unnecessary

Steering is by a conventional Cam Gears rack and pinion system, with the pinion (inclined at 4°) attached to a collapsible steering column carrying two universal joints. Connected by permanently lubricated ball joints (designed to take up play automatically), tie rods extend from each end of the rack to pick up on the front of the wheel uprights.

The rack is geared to give 3.45 turns from lock to lock, and the turning circle is 39ft 3in. (12m). The Testarossa's relative front-end lightness makes power assistance unnecessary. The upper end of the steering column, attached to the bodywork bulkhead by a flexible steel boot, is free to move by means of a lever to give rake adjustment at the steering wheel.

BRAKING SYSTEM AND REAR SUSPENSION

Above: with engine, gearbox and cooling system mounted behind the cockpit, the Testarossa carries a high proportion of its weight (58.7 per cent) over the rear wheels. Rear suspension therefore has unusual arrangement of two sets of integral coil springs and Koni telescopic dampers; by sharing suspension loads, the dampers work efficiently even in the most arduous conditions. Like the front suspension, the rear uses a traditional racing-derived double wishbone set-up, although these members are given extra cross-bracing for strength. The small link rod mounted near the lower end of the rear damper supports an anti-roll bar. Driveshafts are of fixed length and universally jointed. Few production cars have such powerful brakes; these are 12in. ventilated discs (the same size is used at the front) gripped by four-pot calipers located on the trailing edges

BRAKES
Massive strength

Few cars match the strength of the Testarossa's braking system, with its four massive 12in. (310mm) molybdenum cast-iron discs mounted within the wheels. The discs are ventilated by radial internal fins, and they are clasped on their trailing edges by four-pot calipers carrying Galfer 1725FF pads.

Otherwise the system is conventional, with servo assistance (using a Benditalia brake booster), hydraulic operation and separate circuits for front and rear wheels. There is a relief valve,

activated by heavy pedal pressure, on the rear circuit to prevent the back wheels locking under hard braking. The handbrake works by a cable running to two small drum brakes within the rear discs.

WHEELS AND TYRES
Generous dimensions

The Testarossa's distinctive five-spoke alloy wheels, manufactured by Speedline, are of two different sizes. At the rear are 10J × 16in. rims carrying Michelin MXV 255/50 VR 16 tyres, while at the front 8J × 16in. rims are fitted with 225/50

VR 16 tyres – Goodyear NCT Eagle tyres are used on some cars. Normal pressures are 34psi at the front and 37psi at the rear – Ferrari recommend that these are raised to 40psi for running at more than 161mph (260kmh)! The spare wheel, a 115/85 R 18 'spacesaver' mounted in the nose compartment, needs 60psi and is suitable for speeds up to 50mph (80kmh).

Until late 1987, these alloy wheels were located by a single octagonal hub fixing: removal of this with a special spanner and hammer often proved beyond an owner's strength, so Testarossas now have five conventional wheel nuts.

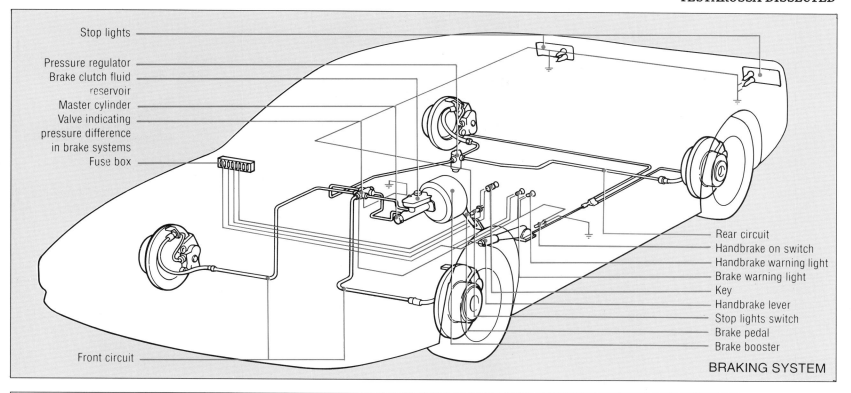

Stop lights
Pressure regulator
Brake clutch fluid reservoir
Master cylinder
Valve indicating pressure difference in brake systems
Fuse box

Rear circuit
Handbrake on switch
Handbrake warning light
Brake warning light
Key
Handbrake lever
Stop lights switch
Brake pedal
Brake booster

Front circuit

BRAKING SYSTEM

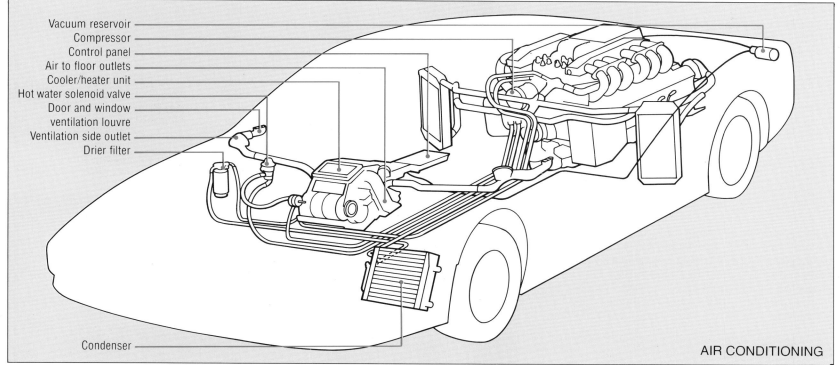

Vacuum reservoir
Compressor
Control panel
Air to floor outlets
Cooler/heater unit
Hot water solenoid valve
Door and window ventilation louvre
Ventilation side outlet
Drier filter

Condenser

AIR CONDITIONING

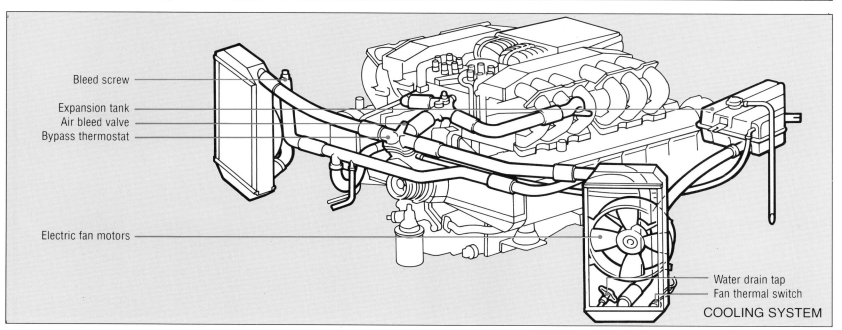

Bleed screw

Expansion tank
Air bleed valve
Bypass thermostat

Electric fan motors

Water drain tap
Fan thermal switch

COOLING SYSTEM

29

BODY AND CHASSIS
Sensational styling from Pininfarina

The Testarossa breaks no new ground in its construction. Like so many Ferraris before it, its chassis is made from square and rectangular section steel tubes welded together into a complex lattice, onto which are hung aluminium and steel panels.

The strongest part of the car is its semi-monocoque cockpit section, from which emerge substantial chassis members to carry the front suspension and rear engine subframes; this latter section can be unbolted for easy engine removal. Aluminium panels are used for all bodywork sections except the doors, roof and bumpers: the doors and roof are made from zinc-coated steel to give extra strength to the passenger cell, and the bumper coverings are glass-reinforced plastic. Glass-fibre liners are fitted to the wheelarches.

Pininfarina's sensational styling makes the Testarossa relatively long at 176.6in. (448.5cm) and immensely wide at 77.8in. (197.6cm); thanks to those huge, slab-like rear wings, the Testarossa is broader than any other car in production today. It is larger than the Boxer in every dimension: it is longer by 3.3in. (8.5cm) and wider by 5.7in. (14.5cm); its 100.4in. (255.0cm) wheelbase is greater by 2.0in. (5.0cm); front track of 59.8in. (151.8cm) is wider by 0.7in. (1.8cm) and rear track has grown by 3.8in. (9.7cm) to 65.4in. (166.0cm).

Much of the purity of the Testarossa's front profile results from moving the water and oil radiators to the car's hips. Without the normal constraints of providing radiator and engine space at the front, the nose is able to sweep down well below the height of the front wheels to a blunt point. There is, in fact, a matt black slatted grille beneath the bumper, but its only purpose is to allow air into ducts leading to the front wheels. The long, off-centre slot in the black chin spoiler is an intake for the air conditioning system.

The entire bonnet area, apart from the retractable headlamp units, lifts with the help of hydraulic struts to reveal a shallow luggage compartment filling the width of the car, but covering only half of the length between nose and windscreen. The bonnet's trailing edge flicks delicately upwards to allow air to pass over the windscreen wipers, and there is a triangular nick on one side to allow the wiper arm to park fully home.

FIVE STRAKES ON A FERRARI
Functionless styling, or . . .?

Those distinctive styling ribs filling the tapered side apertures, leading to the water radiators and oil cooler, are separate steel pressings bolted through the door skins. There are five of them, and the second and fourth are slightly broader than the other three. A vertical black aerofoil panel, broken near its front edge by the door opening, sits within these strakes to help channel air inwards to the radiators. Little door handles are tucked away out of sight, beneath the locks, under the top of these cavernous side openings – you reach under with your fingers and pull towards you.

These strakes met with much adverse comment when the Testarossa was launched, critics saying that such seemingly functionless styling was unworthy of Ferrari. However, it is hard to imagine a more effective solution to smoothing out what otherwise would be a gaping hole.

There is only one fuel filler cap, on the left-hand side as you look from the rear. Two wing mirrors are mounted halfway down the A-posts, although early cars had a single ungainly mirror mounted in

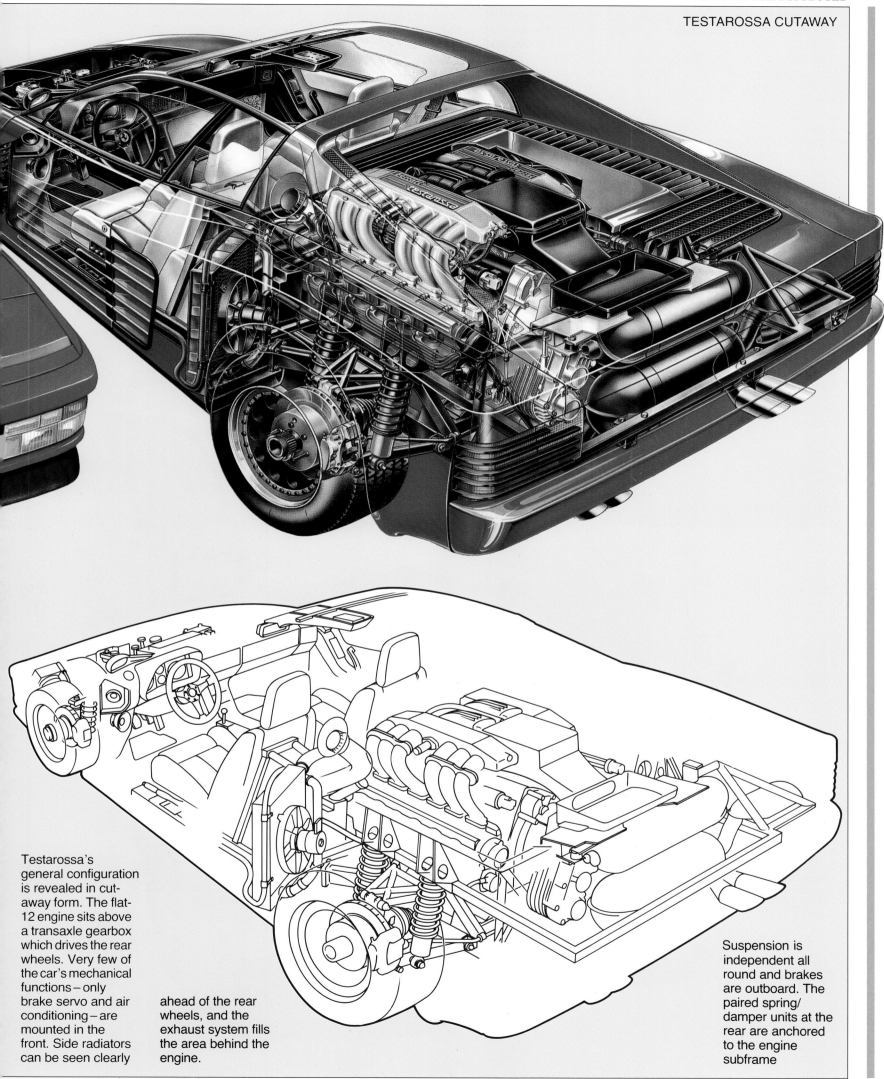

Testarossa's general configuration is revealed in cut-away form. The flat-12 engine sits above a transaxle gearbox which drives the rear wheels. Very few of the car's mechanical functions – only brake servo and air conditioning – are mounted in the front. Side radiators can be seen clearly ahead of the rear wheels, and the exhaust system fills the area behind the engine.

Suspension is independent all round and brakes are outboard. The paired spring/damper units at the rear are anchored to the engine subframe a higher position on the driver's side (see the *Design and Development* chapter for explanation, page 14).

The windscreen is bonded so that it is flush with the roof and side pillars, but the door glasses are secured conventionally in channelled window frames. There is a tiny fixed quarterlight on each side so that the windows can be wound down fully without fouling on the door jambs. The vertical rear window is flat for most of its width, but the ends curve round to form a smooth line into the solid buttresses which extend to the car's tail. This treatment is just like the Dino of 20 years ago.

Most of the car's flat tail section, beneath which the engine can be seen lurking, is covered by a black grille of lateral slats designed to allow hot air to be emitted efficiently. A raised body colour panel covers the central area of this grille to keep rain off the engine itself. The entire tail section, including the side buttresses, is hinged from the roof so that it can lift clear – aided by telescopic struts – to provide excellent engine access.

COOLING REQUIREMENTS
Vents and grilles dominate rear styling
Beneath the slight rising lip at the tail, the back of the car falls off vertically. Above the bumper, another grille of five black horizontal bars, bearing a large Prancing Horse emblem in the centre, gives a pleasing finish to an opening necessary for cooling purposes. Four exhaust pipes, in two pairs either side of a four-bar grille, protrude through the

body colour under-valence.

Pop-up pods, driven by electric motors (although hand-cranking is possible in emergencies), reveal pairs of Carello 55W halogen headlamps, the outer dipped beam units being supplemented by the inner pair on high beam. The rectangular front light clusters below bumper level house parking lights and direction indicators, with thin fog lamps set below them.

Those five black slats across the rear of the car shroud rectangular tail lamp assemblies (the Testarossa is the first Ferrari without traditional circular tail lamps) containing direction indicators, side lights, reversing lights, high-intensity fog lamps and reflectors. European market cars have a single flashing indicator (oddly enough, circular on

some cars and rectangular on others) on each side of the car behind the front wheelarches, whereas US market cars have the obligatory front and rear rectangular side indicators. A further addition for US regulations is a row of small brake lights set centrally into the trailing edge of the engine cover.

All items of detail trim are finished in matt black, as are the shallow sill sections along the car's sides; there is no chrome in sight. Badging is discreet, being confined to a small Testarossa (note, one word!) logo on the tail, Ferrari script on the horizontal rear section just before the tail lip, Pininfarina labels on either side ahead of the rear wheelarches, and a traditional yellow Ferrari badge on the nose.

INTERIOR
Comfort and style
Settle down inside a Testarossa and the first thing that strikes you is the delicious aura created by thoughtful design, English Connolly leather upholstery and Italian wool carpets. It is appreciably more spacious inside than a Boxer, but uncompromisingly a two-seater. Its occupants, however, have plenty of room, and there is a carpeted shelf behind the rear seats to take some of their luggage.

The commonest trim colour combination is three shades of brown: light tan for seats, headlining and door trim; dark siena for fascia and centre console; and mid-brown for the carpets, whose edges are protected by tan leather beading. The seats are beautifully sculpted in smooth leather, with broad padding on their bases and backrests to anchor their occupants during fast cornering. They have electric adjustment, by three buttons on the seat cushion edge facing the door, for backrest fore/aft movement, backrest rake and cushion height. A bar beneath the front of each seat allows manual adjustment for reach. Each seat has a large adjustable head restraint embossed with a Prancing Horse motif.

The front wheelarches intrude considerably into the footwells, but provide convenient places to mount two woofer loudspeakers – two tweeters are recessed into the ends of the fascia. The brake and clutch pedals hinge from above, but the organ-pedal accelerator pivots from the floor. The handbrake sits on the floor between the driver's seat and the door, and adjacent to it are two levers to open the front bonnet lid and rear engine cover.

Although it looks relatively spartan, the fascia is elegantly trimmed in leather, its smooth angled expanses punctuated by stitched seams. In front of the driver is a rectangular instrument binnacle standing proud of the fascia line, in the centre are three air vents and a flap to hide the stereo radio/cassette installation, and ahead of the passenger is a small glovebox (incorporating a vanity mirror) hinged to open downwards. Two further face-level air vents with round 'scallop shell' cover flaps sit at the extreme ends of the fascia, which then curves round to blend into angled pads – containing door handles and small map pockets – along the length of the doors. Extending down from the centre of the fascia is an angular console which bends sharply by the gearlever to form a horizontal channel between the seats. A multitude of dials and switches live in this area.

INSTRUMENTATION
A full complement
Housed within the instrument binnacle are four black Veglia-Borletti dials calibrated in orange. On the left is a 200mph (320kmh for metric markets) electronic speedometer with markings stepped at 5mph (or 10kmh) intervals, and three warning lights for indicators and high beam are set into its bottom segment. On the right is an electronic tachometer reading to 10,000rpm at 250rpm intervals, and red-lined at 6800rpm – warning lights for low fuel and low battery charge are set into a matching bottom segment. Between these two large dials are two smaller gauges indicating oil pressure (with a warning light) and water temperature. Further warning lights along the sides and top edge of the instrument panel are indicators for handbrake release, heated rear window, parking lights, brake circuit failure, open front bonnet lid and open engine cover.

Sprouting from the steering column behind the three-spoke leather-rimmed Momo wheel, complete with a traditional Prancing Horse horn push in the centre, are three finger stalks, two on the left and one on the right. The longer of the left-hand stalks looks after headlamps and dipping, while the shorter one controls the indicators. The right-hand stalk covers the two speeds and intermittent facility of the windscreen wipers, and operates the electric washers. The ignition lock is on the right of the steering column.

Angled towards the driver at the top of the centre console are two more orange-on-black dials, engine oil temperature above fuel level, with further illuminated warnings for front and rear fog lamps alongside them. Continuing down the console, a digital clock with three operating buttons comes next, followed by the mileage and trip recorders which you might have expected to find inset into the speedometer.

At this point, the console bends into its horizontal section, meeting a rectangular cut-out where the gearlever, topped by a black sphere with the shift pattern embossed on it in white, protrudes from the chrome slotted gate – a Maranello hallmark. Adjacent to the gearlever are buttons to activate the windscreen demister, and to switch the

Testarossa's rear 'buttress' styling recalls the 1960s mid-engined Dino, even down to its

curved rear window. Hot air is extracted through the black grilles above and behind the engine

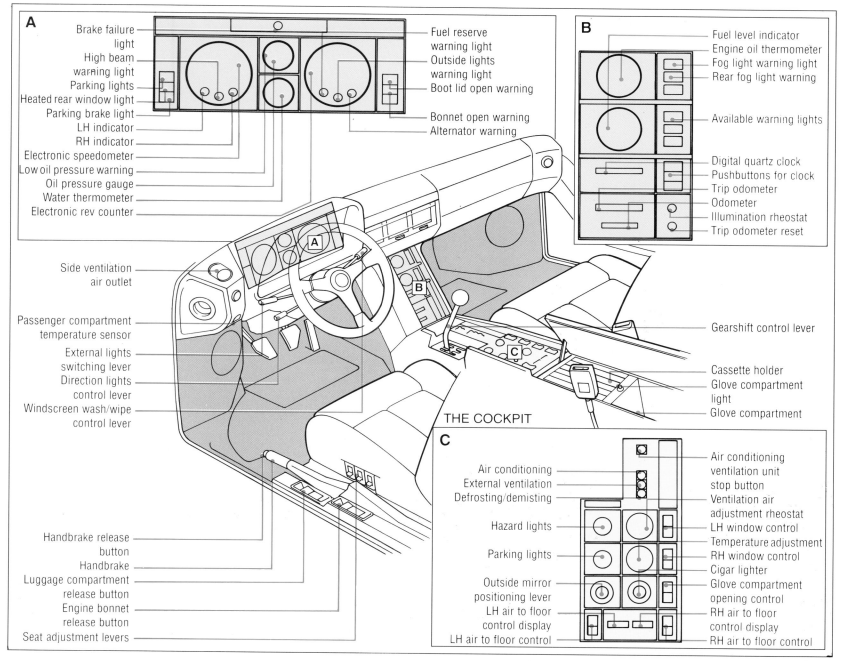

A

- Brake failure light
- High beam warning light
- Parking lights
- Heated rear window light
- Parking brake light
- LH indicator
- RH indicator
- Electronic speedometer
- Low oil pressure warning
- Oil pressure gauge
- Water thermometer
- Electronic rev counter
- Fuel reserve warning light
- Outside lights warning light
- Boot lid open warning
- Bonnet open warning
- Alternator warning

B

- Fuel level indicator
- Engine oil thermometer
- Fog light warning light
- Rear fog light warning
- Available warning lights
- Digital quartz clock
- Pushbuttons for clock
- Trip odometer
- Odometer
- Illumination rheostat
- Trip odometer reset

- Side ventilation air outlet
- Passenger compartment temperature sensor
- External lights switching lever
- Direction lights control lever
- Windscreen wash/wipe control lever

- Gearshift control lever
- Cassette holder
- Glove compartment light
- Glove compartment

THE COCKPIT

- Handbrake release button
- Handbrake
- Luggage compartment release button
- Engine bonnet release button
- Seat adjustment levers

C

- Air conditioning
- External ventilation
- Defrosting/demisting
- Hazard lights
- Parking lights
- Outside mirror positioning lever
- LH air to floor control display
- LH air to floor control
- Air conditioning ventilation unit stop button
- Ventilation air adjustment rheostat
- LH window control
- Temperature adjustment
- RH window control
- Cigar lighter
- Glove compartment opening control
- RH air to floor control display
- RH air to floor control

air conditioning on and off. A panel covered with switches and knobs sits behind the gearlever, containing controls for adjusting air conditioning temperature and fan speed, electric windows and door mirrors, hazard warning lights and a cigar lighter. Right at the tail end of this console sits a padded lid (doubling as an armrest) concealing a small compartment for cassette tapes.

Just in case you are wondering what else can possibly be included in the Testarossa's interior specification, there is also a small roof control panel close to the rear view mirror. Positioned here are buttons for the heated rear window, front and rear fog lamps and interior light, as well as a map-reading spotlight.

The air conditioning system, newly-developed for the Testarossa, comprises a Borletti cooler-heater unit mounted behind the front luggage compartment, a condenser situated in the left-hand front wheelarch, a drying filter positioned by the opposite wheelarch, and a Sankyo compressor driven by belt from the crankshaft. The system, working on pressurised freon gas, keeps the passenger compartment temperature constant when outside condition vary. Air is drawn in from outside through a duct at the nose of the car and, depending on control settings, heated or cooled and/or dehumidified. Cockpit temperature can be adjusted between 18° and 32° C, and the driver and passenger can select different conditions.

The battery is housed under a flap ahead of the right-hand front wheelarch, and access can be gained when the bonnet lid is raised. Mounted on the bulkhead, the fusebox can also be reached when the lid is open.

To emphasise the Testarossa's luggage-carrying advantage over the Boxer, Ferrari commissioned Mauro Schedoni's Modena-based leather company to design a range of special cases for the car. Six pieces, each bearing Testarossa and Prancing Horse motifs, are available in tan hide. Three are shaped to fit in the carpeted front luggage compartment, and three behind the seats. Who needs a Gucci briefcase when you can have Schedoni holdalls? But first you must buy a Testarossa . . .

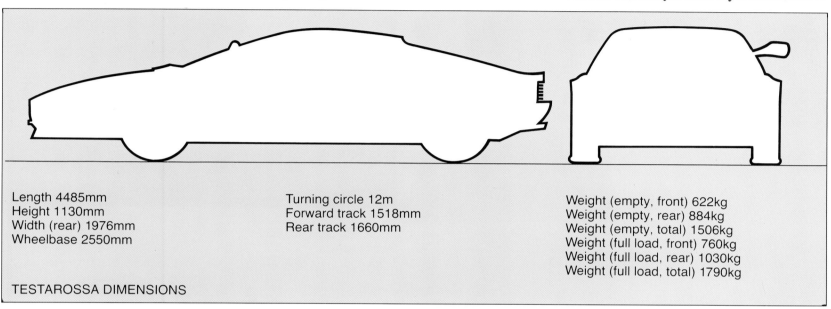

Length 4485mm
Height 1130mm
Width (rear) 1976mm
Wheelbase 2550mm

Turning circle 12m
Forward track 1518mm
Rear track 1660mm

Weight (empty, front) 622kg
Weight (empty, rear) 884kg
Weight (empty, total) 1506kg
Weight (full load, front) 760kg
Weight (full load, rear) 1030kg
Weight (full load, total) 1790kg

TESTAROSSA DIMENSIONS

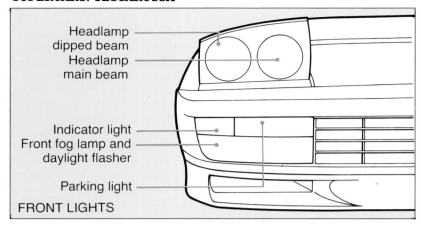

Headlamp dipped beam
Headlamp main beam

Indicator light
Front fog lamp and daylight flasher

Parking light

FRONT LIGHTS

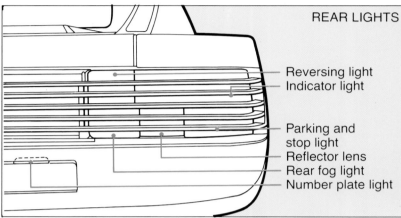

REAR LIGHTS

Reversing light
Indicator light

Parking and stop light
Reflector lens
Rear fog light
Number plate light

POWER CURVE

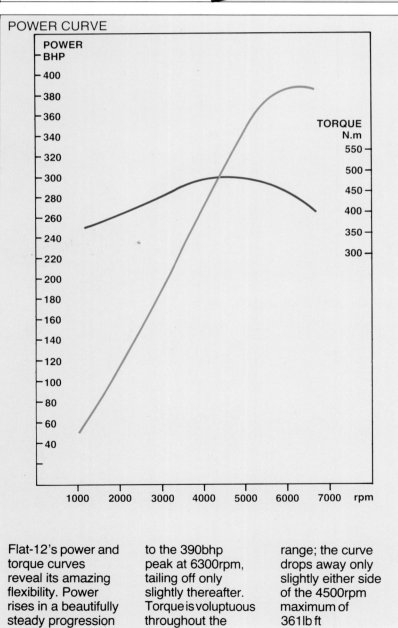

Flat-12's power and torque curves reveal its amazing flexibility. Power rises in a beautifully steady progression to the 390bhp peak at 6300rpm, tailing off only slightly thereafter. Torque is voluptuous throughout the range; the curve drops away only slightly either side of the 4500rpm maximum of 361lb ft

FERRARI TESTAROSSA
Specifications

Engine	Configuration	Flat-12, horizontally opposed at 180°, mounted behind cockpit, type F113A
	Construction	All-alloy
	Capacity	4942cc (301.5cu in.)
	Bore	82mm (3.20in.)
	Stroke	78mm (3.04in.)
	Compression ratio	9.3:1
	Main bearings	Seven
	Max. engine speed	6800rpm
	Normal idle speed	1000rpm ± 100rpm
	Maximum power	390bhp (286.8KW) at 6300rpm
	Specific power	78.9bhp/litre (58KW/litre)
	Maximum torque	361.6lb ft (490.3Nm)
	Firing order	1-9-5-12-3-8-6-10-2-7-4-11
	Fiscal rating (Italy)	36CV
	Valve gear	Four per cylinder, driven by two overhead camshafts (one intake, one exhaust) per bank
	Valve inclination	20° inlet, 21° exhaust
	Camshaft drive	Toothed Goodyear Supertorque PD rubber belts
	Intake timing	Opens 13° BTDC, closes 51° ABDC
	Exhaust timing	Opens 54° BBDC, closes 10° ATDC
Cooling	Type	Closed-circuit water-cooled
	Radiators	Two Puma-Chausson side-mounted radiators carrying thermostatically-controlled Spal electric fans switching in at 84°C, switching out at 75°C
	Capacity	20 litres (4.4 gallons) of water/antifreeze mixture pressurised at 0.9kg/cm² (12.8psi)
Fuel system	Type	Two Bosch KE-Jetronic mechanical injection systems (one per bank)
	Fuel delivery	Two Bosch electric pumps
	Fuel capacity	Two light-alloy tanks totalling 115 litres (25.3 gallons) plus 18 litre reserve (3.9 gallons)

Electrics	Ignition system	Marelli Microplex MED 120B computerised electronic ignition
	Ignition advance	8° at 1000rpm, 30° at 5000rpm
	Spark plugs	Champion A6G
	Plug size	12mm × 1.25mm
	Plug gap	0.6mm–0.7mm (0.024in.–0.028in.)
	Coils	Two Marelli AEI 500C
	Alternator	AC Delco 120A
	Battery	66Ah 12V AC Delco DR765
	Starter motor	Bosch
Lubrication	Type	Dry sump system with separate oil tank and radiator, scavenge pump and pressure pump
	Oil capacity	15.5 litres (27 pints)
	Idle oil pressure	4.5kg/cm^2 (64.0psi)
	Max. oil pressure	6.5kg/cm^2 (92.5psi)
	Recommended oil	Agip Sint 2000 SAE 10W50
Transmission	Gearbox	Five-speed in unit with final drive, all-synchromesh by floating rings
	Oil capacity	9.5 litres (17 pints)
	Recommended oil	Agip Rotra MP SAE 80W90
	First gear/ mph per 1000rpm	3.139:1/7.4mph
	Second gear/ mph per 1000rpm	2.014:1/11.5mph
	Third gear/ mph per 1000rpm	1.526:1/15.2mph
	Fourth gear/ mph per 1000rpm	1.167:1/19.8mph
	Fifth gear/ mph per 1000rpm	0.875:1/26.5mph
	Reverse ratio	2.532:1
	Final drive	Hypoid bevel gears with ZF limited slip differential
	Final drive ratio	3.21:1 (45:14 reduction ratio)
	Clutch	Borg & Beck 9½in. (242mm) dry double-plate, hydraulically actuated
Suspension	Front	Independent by double wishbones, coil springs, Koni 82P 2279 shock absorbers, anti-roll bar, rubber bump and rebound blocks
	Rear	Independent by braced double wishbones, paired coil springs, paired Koni 82P 2142 shock absorbers, anti-roll bar, rubber bump and rebound blocks
Steering	Type	Cam Gears rack and pinion, symmetrical track rods
	Ratio	3.45 turns lock to lock
	Rack full stroke	13.0cm (5.07in.)
	Turning circle	12.0m (39.3ft)
Brakes	System	Hydraulic servo-assisted front/rear split dual circuit
	Front	12in. (310mm) ventilated discs with four-pot calipers
	Rear	12in. (310mm) ventilated discs with four-pot calipers
	Pads	Galfer 1725FF
	Handbrake	Cable-operated to rear wheel drums
Wheels/tyres	Front rims	Speedline five-spoke alloy, 8J × 16in.
	Front tyres	225/50 VR 16 (Michelin MXV or Goodyear Eagle NCT)
	Front pressure	2.4 bar (34psi)
	Front camber angle	0°–0° 15′
	Front toe-in	0.5mm–1.0mm (0.02in.–0.04in.)
	Front caster angle	5° 30′
	Kingpin angle	11° 30′
	Rear rims	Speedline five-spoke alloy, 10J × 16in.
	Rear tyres	255/50 VR 16 (Michelin MXV or Goodyear Eagle NCT)
	Rear pressure	2.5 bar (37psi)
	Rear wheel camber	−0° 45′ – −1°
	Rear wheel toe-in	0.5mm–1.0mm (0.02in.–0.04in.)
	Spare wheel	3.25in. Bx 18 alloy 'spacesaver' rim (maximum speed 50mph)
	Spare tyre	115/80 R 18 (Michelin or Goodyear)
	Spare pressure	4.2 bar (60psi)
Structure	Chassis	Tubular steel with central monocoque section
	Body	Aluminium body panels, with doors and roof section in zinc-treated steel (Zincrox), bumpers in glass-reinforced plastic
Dimensions	Length	448.5cm (176.5in.)
	Width	197.6cm (77.8in.)
	Height	113.0cm (44.5in.)
	Wheelbase	255.0cm (100.4in.)
	Front track	151.8cm (59.8in.)
	Rear track	166.0cm (65.4in.)
	Kerb weight	1506kg (3320lb)
Performance[1]	Maximum speed	180.2mph (290kmh)
	0–62.1mph (100kmh)	5.8 sec
	0–400m	13.6sec
	Standing kilometre	24.1 sec
Performance[2]	Maximum speed	180.1mph
	Maximum in fourth	137.0mph
	Maximum in third	105.0mph
	Maximum in second	79.0mph
	Maximum in first	51.0mph
	0–30mph	2.6sec
	0–40mph	3.4sec
	0–50mph	4.3sec
	0–60mph	5.8sec
	0–70mph	7.1sec
	0–80mph	8.8sec
	0–90mph	10.6sec
	0–100mph	12.7sec
	0–110mph	15.5sec
	0–120mph	18.2sec
	Standing quarter-mile	14.2sec
	20–40mph (in 5th)	6.9sec
	20–40mph (in 4th)	4.5sec
	30–50mph (in 5th)	6.9sec
	30–50mph (in 4th)	4.4sec
	40–60mph (in 5th)	6.8sec
	40–60mph (in 4th)	4.4sec
	50–70mph (in 5th)	7.3sec
	50–70mph (in 4th)	4.5sec
	60–80mph (in 5th)	8.0sec
	60–80mph (in 4th)	4.6sec
	70–90mph (in 5th)	8.9sec
	70–90mph (in 4th)	4.7sec
	80–100mph (in 5th)	10.0sec
	80–100mph (in 4th)	4.9sec
Consumption	Urban cycle	12.2mpg
	At 56mph	28.3mpg
	At 75mph	24.8mpg

[1]Official Ferrari figures.
[2]Figures obtained by *Motor* magazine published 13 July 1985.
All other specifications as issued by Ferrari.

MANUFACTURE

Following the Testarossa through its construction stages as it takes shape at Pininfarina and Maranello

BEFORE A TESTAROSSA even turns a wheel under its own power it has made several journeys, for the cars are built in stages at three premises. ITCA builds Testarossa bodies and chassis in Turin; Pininfarina paints and trims them; and at Maranello all the major mechanical parts are made and assembled to complete the cars. This process differs from the bulk of Ferrari production, as the manufacture of V8-engined cars is carried out entirely in-house.

FIRST STEPS
Body panels and chassis
ITCA, based close to Pininfarina, is a small concern working solely for Ferrari on prototype and low-volume production. Employing highly-skilled staff, it is a traditional company where the emphasis is on craftsmanship – beating the Testarossa's aluminium body panels and welding up its chassis are operations carried out by hand.

The chassis is made from square and rectangular section steel tubing, onto which is mounted aluminium and steel panelling. Each bodyshell, or body-in-white, leaves ITCA with bonnet and doors in place, but with the side strakes hung within the car. Although most of the Testarossa's body is made from aluminium, traditionally used by coachbuilders because it is light and easy to work, the doors and roof are steel in the interests of greater impact resistance. To say that they are steel, however, is a simplification, for Ferrari specifies a specially treated steel called zincrox.

Zincrox was developed by Ferrari in 1981, and now all its steel-bodied cars are made from this material. Like all Italian car manufacturers, Ferrari had been forced to conquer corrosion during the 1970s, and its metallurgists came up with a patented process to coat steel panels with a combination of zinc, chrome and chrome oxide. Zincrox costs 20 per cent more to produce than conventional steel, but its value was proved after more than 1000 hours of testing in corrosive salt chambers.

AT PININFARINA
Joining the line
When they arrive at Pininfarina's Grugliasco factory, these body/chassis units are wheeled to the beginning of new priming and painting lines, to join all the other Lancia, Alfa Romeo, Peugeot and Cadillac models which the company produces on a sub-contract basis. The first section in this long process, which sees each bodyshell pass up and down a series of lines totalling 400 yards in length, is the Pininfarina Phosphate System.

As a car enters this enclosed line, a high-pressure spray (containing water and solvents) first removes grease from its surface. The car is then rinsed with pure water before the next step of zinc-phosphate immersion, a unique – and secret – Pininfarina-patented process which can treat steel, aluminium and zinc (the three metals in a Testarossa bodyshell) at the same time. Previously, aluminium bodies had to pass down a separate preparation line.

There are another two rinses in deionised water after the zinc-phosphate layer (an anti-corrosive coating which also provides a good paint key) has been applied, and then each bodyshell passes through a drying oven. From here, the car emerges dry, hot and clean to make a U-turn into the first catophoretic bath, comprising anti-corrosive primer diluted with water; this mixture is electrically-charged so that every crevice of the body is penetrated. The bodyshell rises out of this into a curing oven, and then receives two more primer coats.

Still the car has yet to receive its body colour. Now finished in a matt orange primer, the bodyshell is ready to have all its internal panel joins sealed with PVC, and plastic underseal is applied. All through this process, the Testarossa's treatment is identical to that of the other cars on the line, but then comes the quality control point where the supercar is singled out for special attention, and for careful rubbing back of the primer coats to create a perfect surface for final painting.

AUTOMATIC PAINTING
Culmination of patented process
Once the bodyshell is sufficiently smooth, it goes onto Pininfarina's new automatic electrostatic painting line (completed at the end of 1987) for a final primer coat. As the paint leaves the spray nozzles, it is charged to 6000V so that it is electrostatically attracted to the bodyshell – this produces a more even surface than manual spraying, although inaccessible areas, like door shut faces, still have to be sprayed by hand.

All this is carried out within glass cells beneath which water circulates fiercely to extract

Testarossa bodyshell emerges from initial catophoretic bath, *left*, with its first coat of anti-corrosive primer

Bodyshell passes through a drying oven, *above*, after deionised water rinses and zinc-phosphate process

impurities, which could settle in the paint, from the atmosphere. At last, after a remarkable preparation process, the top layer of Glasurit acrylic body colour – comprising a laqueur coat on top of the paint – is applied, and dried in an oven.

So far, each embryonic Testarossa has taken about a day to go through the automated painting stages. The shiny new bodyshell, now with a hand-sprayed matt black interior, receives protective plastic coverings for vulnerable areas before being transferred through a tunnel to the trimming line.

Here it will spend another three days acquiring all the internal and external trim pieces which turn it gradually from a slightly anonymous painted shell into something that begins to resemble a finished car. Alongside the trimming line's thirteen stations is a small warehouse of parts – glass, leather panels, rubber insulation strips, instruments, wiring, lights and so on – largely brought in from outside suppliers.

The stages of the trimming process are carefully organised so that each bodyshell, mounted to a conveyor belt, spends around two hours at each station. The windscreen, windows and some of the wiring systems are fitted at stage 1. More wiring, rubber hoses and window frames go on at stage 2, and badges and windscreen wipers are added at stage 3. Stage 4 sees some of the body trim pieces – side strakes, mirrors and black louvres – put in place, and stage 5 is occupied with fitting more electrical systems, horns and brake servo.

The first attention to the interior comes at stage 6 with the installation of sound-deadening felt on the bare cockpit floor and the air conditioning system. Stage 7 is taken up with the complex job of fitting electric window mechanisms to both doors, adding hydraulic supporting struts to the bonnet lid, a fuel filler lock, rubber sealing strips, headlamp pods and bumpers.

Through stage 8, the interior begins to take shape, gaining first the pedals and centre console. Then comes the rest of the fascia, seat belts, and rear shelf trim at stage 9. Front and rear bumpers are fitted at stage 10, together with interior carpeting. The steering column, heater system, handbrake and boot and bonnet cables go in at stage 11, leaving just the remaining interior items – steering column, door trim, control stalks, seats and instrument panel (supplied as a complete unit by Veglia-Borletti) – to be fitted at stage 12.

The last stage comprises a few final items, like steering wheel and gear knob, as well as a check to ensure that all the electrical systems are working. This is where quality is given a final assessment. In case the bodywork has suffered any blemishes during the trimming process, there is a separate spray booth and oven for paint rectification.

As the cars go down the line, it is interesting to observe that each one carries a label bearing the customer's name and destination country. With a waiting list of a year, almost every Testarossa is pre-sold. The nationality identification is vital, as each country's Type Approval requirements vary. At the end of the line, two A4 sheets of typewritten instructions outline these differences, which must be checked on each car before it is despatched to Maranello: for example US and Swiss market cars take unleaded fuel only, and British cars need a dim-dip headlamp facility. The customer identification also allows any non-standard requirements – such as different seats, or a unique interior trim colour – to be met.

Orange primer coat is rubbed back, *below*, before final acrylic colour layers are applied; good preparation is essential here

Strakes, *right*, are bolted home on trim line. Interior takes shape, *below right*, with instruments, fascia and centre console in place

By this point the Testarossa has blossomed into a fully-trimmed bodyshell, and it is time for the 150 mile journey to Maranello. Pininfarina's backlog of 'stock' is typically around thirty Testarossas, enough to supply Ferrari for nearly two weeks. A closed truck calls two or three times a week to carry away the finished bodyshells.

TO MARANELLO
Final assembly
A tiny part of Maranello's total factory area – only 10 per cent – is devoted to the final assembly of cars on four production lines. The allocation of these lines varies according to Ferrari's model mix, but one is always devoted to Testarossas (with a few V12-engined 412i saloons passing through as well). As this is written, the F40 has one line, and the 328GTB/GTS range – the vast bulk of Ferrari's production – occupies the other two.

Testarossas arrive at the beginning of their line just as they left Pininfarina, as fully-trimmed bodyshells. The final assembly process begins with the fitting of braking and cooling system pipework, water and oil radiators behind the side air intakes, a pair of Spal electric fans to cool the radiators, and

the two fuel tanks inserted between engine and bulkhead.

All this takes place before the car's first move down the production line to the second station, where a complete engine/gearbox/rear suspension assembly is manoeuvred into position below the engine bay. This unit, already cradled in its chassis subframe, arrives from another part of the factory ready to be installed by one man. The whole assembly is raised on a hydraulic lift until four mounting plates align with their attachment points on the bulkhead. There are also mounting points above each of the four rear shock absorbers, and another pair in the back of the wheelarches. The hydraulic lift can be positioned very precisely, but it is incongruous to see a crowbar used to help the engine home! In just half an hour the installation is complete.

From here, the car travels forwards onto an elevated line, a scaffolding structure raised eight feet off the ground to enable comfortable access to the underside of each car. There is also a narrow walkway either side of this platform. Five Testarossas are completed daily, and each takes three days to emerge as a finished car.

Completed body-shells at Pininfarina's Grugliasco factory, *above*, waiting for the truck which will take them to Maranello for final mechanical assembly

Lowering the engine, *above right*, into its subframe, with rear suspension already fitted. Complete engine ready to be mounted, *below right*, in bodyshell

Once on this platform, the Testarossa looks almost complete, needing just final touches. Front suspension, front brakes, exhaust system, steering rack, wheels and tyres are the obvious items to be fitted, but there is plenty of detailed attention too. Sound and heat absorbing materials – comprising aluminium-backed fibre panels – are positioned on the bulkhead between engine and cockpit.

At the end of the line the car drops back to floor level to have its wheel geometry adjusted on Hunter computerised *geometria ruote* equipment, and all the lighting and electrical equipment is checked. Extractor fan ducts are then fitted over the exhaust, and the engine started so that the car may be driven under its own power for the first time.

THE FOUNDRY
Moulds and metal

Ferrari is unusual, especially for such a small manufacturer, in having its own foundry. A thundering oven of a place, this is where virtually all of the flat-12's engine, gearbox and suspension castings – and those for the V8 and V12 engines of the other models – are made. Magnesium components for racing engines are also cast here.

Ferrari employs metallurgists to study and modify its alloys, and also to check samples for quality by spectroscopic analysis. The alloy used in all engines nowadays comprises 90 per cent aluminium, 9.4 per cent silicon and a remaining 0.6 per cent made up of traces of iron, magnesium, manganese, titanium and copper.

Everything is traditionally sand-cast in moulding boxes, which have to be prepared anew every time they are used. The male and female sides of the moulds are coated with a layer of moistened and hardened sand and clay to keep the casting and mould from fusing together – just like greasing a baking tray. It is this sand that gives the finished engine parts their sparkling external texture.

Molten aluminium heated to 600°C – *Dottore* Pietro de Franchi, Ferrari's Public Relations Director, calls this a 'James Bond Cocktail'! – is drawn from furnaces below ground level, and poured into the moulding boxes. After being left for an hour to allow the liquid aluminium to set, the moulding boxes are vibrated to free the new castings. They fall out as rough pieces covered in flash, just like parts from an Airfix kit.

Most of the workers in the foundry are engaged in the continuous process of preparing the moulding boxes, some of which are very complicated. For example, a cylinder head has to be made up of one large mould into which are cemented separate pieces to form the shape for each exhaust and inlet passage – 24 per head.

Molten aluminium at 600°C, *below* and *below right*, is poured into moulding boxes to form engine and transmission castings

Parts for sand-casting, like cylinder head moulds, have to be carefully prepared by hand, *right*, in the Maranello foundry

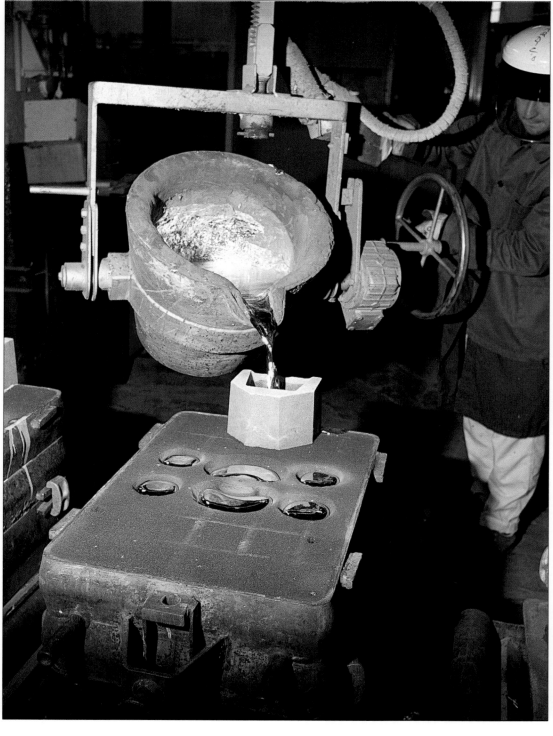

COMPUTERISED MACHINING
'The Green Giants'

The rough castings are then transferred to an area which Ferrari calls its Flexible Manufacturing System (FMS), a fully-automated machining process. These computerised machines, mostly made by Mandelli of Piacenza, run twenty-four hours a day, and can be operated by one man.

Ferrari claim that this is the most modern system of its kind in Europe, and one of the first in the world. Its construction began in 1983, and now it is close to completion. Each machining unit has a programmed drill which takes its tools automatically from a looped rack, and the piece to be worked sits on a revolving plinth. Over the course of an hour or so, a rough casting for a cylinder head,

Testarossa crank-case, *top*, is machined by computer control at one of Maranello's row of FMS, *right*, stations. Checks, as on this crankshaft, *above*, are carried out by micrometer and human eye

crankcase or gearbox casing is turned into a finished piece. Samples are occasionally taken to have their tolerances checked by micrometer.

Almost all engine and gearbox castings, therefore, are produced in-house. Perhaps the most significant exception is the crankshaft, cast outside Maranello from a solid billet of KNV steel. Once its molecular structure has settled, it is machined in Maranello; the tolerances of *every* finished crankshaft are checked by micrometer.

ENGINE ASSEMBLY
The redhead emerges

All the machined parts are taken on trolleys to the engine assembly area, close to the final assembly lines. V8s far outnumber flat-12s, but a close look shows one small U-shaped assembly line where these massive engines, with their distinctive red cam covers, take shape.

Work begins with a bare aluminium crankcase, into which the main bearings, crankshaft and cylinder liners are fitted. Then come the pistons, con rods and big end bearings. Each cylinder head, with its pair of steel camshafts and twenty-four valves (from Eaton, an English company), is

assembled separately before being mounted as a completed unit to the crankcase. Work on the cylinder heads is highly skilled, and it is a joy to watch a man locating the cast iron valve seats gently by hammer, for only by sound and touch can this job be done properly.

The next stage – the moment when the Testarossa takes its name – is to add the crackle-finish red cam covers. By now the engine is looking close to its final form, with only intake and exhaust manifolds, fuel injection and ancillaries left to be fitted. Gearbox/differential units, having been assembled on an adjacent line, also arrive at this point to be mated to the bottom of the engine.

Stages in engine assembly include the 'redhead' going on, *above*, crankcase assembly, *top right*, and 24-valve head fitting, *below right*. Cutaway engine exposes some parts, *far right*

Each completed engine is run in one of Ferrari's five test cells for four hours before being approved for installation in a Testarossa; all the same, an owner is recommended to run-in his new Testarossa in the usual way. The test begins with slow-speed running at 1500rpm, and builds gradually up to a five minute burst at 6300rpm to check that the correct maximum power output can

be achieved. Torque, fuel consumption, temperature and oil pressure readings must also reach the required standard.

Roughly one engine in ten is given an exhaustive twelve hour run as part of the quality control procedure, and if anything is amiss there are said to be 'major repercussions'. Faults are rare, substandard engines being found only around once a year . . .

THE FINISHING SHOP
A last look
After all the hubbub of Ferrari's manufacturing areas, the finishing shop is tranquil. Brightly lit,

spotlessly clean and air conditioned, this hall is like a hospital ward the size of a football pitch. Here detailed attention is given to all completed cars, and quality control inspectors check them after their 125 mile road evaluation. Cleanliness is so important that there is even a vibrating doormat at the entrance to scrub the soles of your shoes . . .

Each car, by now wearing a coat of grime accumulated on the road test, moves slowly forwards on a conveyor belt, and is thoroughly cleaned by a high-pressure airline with what looks like a shaving brush on the end of it. Since all the mechanical quality control has been carried out during the road test, the attention here is centred

on cosmetic appearance. The quality control staff have a scrupulous eye for paint defects, marking every blemish – some are barely visible – with blue chinagraph pencil.

Many of the workers (half of them are female here) are occupied with fine paint brushes and rubber sealant applicators. Windscreen and window glasses are given a waterproof seal, small paint blemishes are rectified by brush (or spray if a large area has to be covered), the interior is cleaned, Tuff-Kote Dinol rust protection is applied to internal sections, and each car is waxed and polished before receiving a final wax coating to protect it on the journey to the customer.

THE FERRARI FACTORY
A story of rapid growth

Considering that Ferrari produced just 3942 cars–of which between 600 and 700 were Testarossas–in 1987, the Maranello factory is an astonishingly large and modern facility. Although the façade you see from the main Modena–Abetone road, passing right by the factory gates, has changed little in 30 years, beyond it lies a huge complex of buildings which has expanded considerably in the last 15 years.

First, a few facts about the size of Ferrari. Today it produces more cars than at any stage in its history, and around 80 per cent are exported to twenty-one countries. Over the last 40 years, around 45,000 cars (as many as Fiat produces in eight days!) have left its gates, and about 70 per cent still survive. Annual turnover is close to 300 billion lire (about £143 million) and profit runs at around 15 billion lire (about £7 million) a year. Approximately 15 per cent of turnover is currently invested annually in plant modernisation and research. Around 1750 people are employed at two sites – the Maranello factory and the Scaglietti body works in Modena. A further 200 are employed by the Racing Department just to design, develop and run two Grand Prix cars. Ferrari's two factories occupy a total area of 1,593,000sq ft, 775,000sq ft of which is covered.

Enzo Ferrari laid the basis of this great company during World War II. He had already carved a fine reputation before the war, first as a racing driver during the 1920s (among his successes was second place on the 1920 Targa Florio) and then as a team manager during the 1930s, running works Alfa Romeos under the Scuderia Ferrari banner. When the war came he set up a machine tool business in Modena making hydraulic grinding machines for ball bearing production, and soon his reputation grew in this new field.

In 1943, when he was employing 150 people, orders came from Mussolini's fascist regime that industry should decentralise into the countryside as protection against allied bombing. Ferrari owned a small villa and some land at Maranello, close to the Appennine foothills ten miles south of Modena, and it was here that he relocated his business, turning his thoughts at the same time to car production once the war was over. Despite two bombing raids in November 1944 and February 1945 – some spent British machine gun rounds were found only a few years ago during repair work to the old Racing Department roof! – he was well placed at armistice, with a new factory and a good workforce, to achieve his aims.

A medium-sized industrial city, Modena was to become the focus of the exotic car world over the next 30 years. Ferrari started here, Maserati moved into the city from Bologna, and Lamborghini and de Tomaso are close by. In his autobiography, *Le Mie Gioie Terribili* (*My Terrible Joys*), Ferrari explains why Modena, and the Emilia-Romagna region around it, are so special.

It is an area of '. . . small and medium concerns with an incredible variety of activities and products . . . large plants have made no headway in Emilia-Romagna, whereas I have seen an enormous vitality in those enterprises which emanate from the family group, spreading as oil does on water . . .' He describes its people as '. . . an intelligent, willing, technically prepared workforce, traditionally capable. It is a fact that here in Emilia-Romagna people have always nourished a love for technical education; in this there is a real tradition . . . Here one does not first build factories and then look for manpower – no, here we first form men by making available the necessary technical know-how and then we erect the factories. A factory is first and foremost made of people, then of machinery and, lastly, of bricks and mortar . . .'

As Ferrari concentrated on a lavish racing programme after the war, series production of his hand-made, expensive *Gran Turismo* cars grew slowly, not passing 100 units a year until 1957. It was the Dino of 1966 that moved the company into a bigger league, annual production reaching 1000 in 1971 and climbing above 2000 in 1979. Today the target is to approach 4000 cars a year, but to go no further.

Ferrari knows that scarcity feeds the mystique of its cars. Unlike Porsche, its senior management is so imbued with the need for exclusivity that it will always seek to preserve its happy position where demand outstrips supply. As *Ingegnere* Giovanni Sguazzini, Ferrari President until the end of 1985, told me a few years ago, 'The factory is capable of producing more cars, but we know our limit. We would be sacrificing our high quality to go much further.'

A NEW LANDMARK
Fiat acquires 50 per cent of Ferrari

The biggest landmark in Ferrari's history came with the Fiat buy-in of 1969. Ferrari was in some financial trouble at the time, and Fiat staved off Ford's approaches with a financial package which resulted in the Italian giant (Lancia, Alfa Romeo and Autobianchi also shelter under the Fiat umbrella) acquiring 50 per cent of Ferrari. Fiat, a world leader in robotic car production, has been the source of the investment needed to modernise Maranello, and production has almost quadrupled during its guardianship. Some of Ferrari's most senior management have arrived from Fiat, including Giovanni Battista Razelli, the current *Direttore Generale*.

As a result of this investment, Ferrari is now an intriguing blend of automated sophistication and traditional craftsmanship. While the factory's Mandelli machine tools mean that most engine parts are made without human touch, their assembly remains a highly skilled, painstaking job, carried out by both men and women. Enzo Ferrari once considered women 'a disruptive influence', but now more than 10 per cent of the workforce is female. Everyone working in the factory seems content, as if working for Ferrari really is the fulfilment of a dream.

Most of the staff work an 8.00a.m. to 5.00p.m. shift with an hour off for lunch. One of the most exciting sights during the day is the stampede to the canteen – restaurant would be a far better word in view of the superb food served there – situated across the main road which divides the factory from the

Racing Department. The only parts of the factory which operate at night are the foundry and the computerised machining systems.

Today, Modena is the Vatican of the motor industry. So evident is the Ferrari name that visiting the city is like making a pilgrimage: shops, garages, bars and restaurants are full of reminders – flags, stickers, posters, photographs – that you are somewhere special. Even the Modena telephone directory contains hundreds of Ferraris, but then the name, which translates as Smith, is one of the commonest in Italy . . .

And Enzo Ferrari is the motor industry's Pope. He had just passed his 90th birthday as this was written, and, clichéd though it is, he is indeed a legend in his own lifetime. Although he was born before the first aeroplane flew, he still controls the company he founded when he was 49, an age when many men would be looking towards retirement. Despite having lived almost as long as the automobile itself, his passion for his cars – Grand Prix machines as well as production models – is undiminished.

'The most exciting thing in my life,' he told me in an interview in 1983, 'is being able to create something living from raw materials.

From nothing arises something useful. Building a car is like bringing up a son. You teach and feed him with great care so that one day you may say with pride: "He is my son." '

THE PININFARINA FACTORY
Manufacturing alongside style

Considering that Pininfarina produces no cars bearing its own name, the size of its main factory, at Grugliasco, a suburb of Turin, is staggering, covering 1,673,800sq ft. In among all the Alfa Romeo Spiders, Peugeot 205 Cabriolets, Lancia Thema Estates and Cadillac Allantés which it is sub-contracted to build, the sight of a Testarossa is indeed rare.

Pininfarina, one of several such coachbuilding companies in Italy, has no parallel in Britain and the USA, although its manufacturing output is close in scale to Jaguar's. The only model ever to have been marketed as a Pininfarina car is the Spidereuropa of 1982–6, but this was merely a rebadged version of the Fiat 124 Spider which Pininfarina had been building since 1966.

Today, Pininfarina has two newer premises besides its Grugliasco base. Since 1982, all styling and design has been based at *Studi e Ricerche*, a striking modern building at Cambiano, twenty miles east of Turin, and extra manufacturing capacity to assemble Cadillac Allantés was opened in 1986 at San Giorgio Canavese, near Turin airport. One of the most important facilities Pininfarina has at Grugliasco is its full-scale wind tunnel chamber, which was the first in Italy when it was built in 1972.

THE 'f' PLAN
A prolific relationship

It has always been a family business. It was founded as Carrozzeria Pinin Farina in 1930 by Battista Farina (nicknamed 'Pinin' because he was small), who previously had worked for his brother Giovanni's bodyshop, Stabilimenti Farina. Pinin was starting out on his own in a business he knew well, that of building special bodies, but he wanted to expand it beyond a craftsman's activity into an independent industry designing and manufacturing on behalf of other manufacturers. The company today fulfils exactly those earliest aims.

Although Pininfarina has designed far more cars than it has manufactured, those which it has built have invariably originated in its own styling studios. Classic examples over the years have been Lancia Aurelia B20 (1951), Nash Healey (1952), Fiat 124 Spider (1966), Lancia Beta Monte Carlo (1975) and Lancia Gamma Coupé (1976). Pininfarina has enjoyed a close and prolific relationship with Maranello since its first Ferrari, the 212 Inter Cabriolet of 1952, and Ferrari has not employed another design agency since Bertone's 308GT4 of 1973.

Since Pininfarina in a sense acts as safety-valve production capacity for larger car companies, its manufacturing output has always fluctuated. Production peaks have often been followed by troughs: a volume of 19,864 in 1963 was followed by only 10,493 in 1965, and a peak of 26,607 in 1979 dropped to 12,147 by 1981. In the last few years the level has been over 30,000.

Pininfarina has always remained in family hands, and today's chairman, Sergio Pininfarina, is the founder's son. The third generation also works in the company: one of Sergio's sons, Andrea, is Joint General Manager (with his father) at *Studi e Ricerche*; another son, Paolo, works at *Studi e Ricerche*; and Sergio's daughter, Lorenza, works in the Public Relations Department.

Pinin Farina, incidentally, merged his name into one word in 1961, but the company's badge has retained its 'f' motif to this day.

DRIVING IMPRESSIONS

Experiencing on the road sensations of driving the Testarossa, one of the world's most capable supercars

I WELL REMEMBER my immense surprise when I first drove a Testarossa. With memories of a 512BBi relatively fresh, I expected the Testarossa to be something similar, only larger, more powerful, faster and even more highly strung. I felt sure that it would be a challenge to master, just as the great supercar Ferraris of the past have been.

Like, I suspect, almost everyone else who has driven a Testarossa with pre-conceived notions, I was greatly surprised by it. Of course, it is awesomely quick and handles brilliantly, but it achieves its statuesque performance with such ease, grace and composure that it is a remarkably undemanding car to drive. As one Ferrari man told me in forewarning, 'Even your granny could drive a Testarossa'.

So strong is the aura of the Prancing Horse that Ferrari does not need motoring magazine road tests and journalists' driving impressions to help sell its cars. Maranello Concessionaires Ltd in Britain is typical of Ferrari's export distributors throughout the world in almost deliberately preserving the mystique of its cars. Every other car manufacturer, even those as small as Rolls-Royce and Lotus, maintains a small fleet of its models for journalists to assess. Even if the reported verdicts are not always as rosy as manufacturers would like, publicity itself is half the aim.

But Ferrari is the maverick of the car business, and needs no one else to tell the world how good its cars are. Maranello Concessionaires Ltd sells virtually all the 250 or so Ferraris it imports in an average year with only the factory's test mileage on the clock. A handful do a little more in the course of gentle demonstrations to prospective buyers, but there has very rarely been a car available for magazines to evaluate. Ferrari just is not interested in having its performance figures confirmed by the computerised speed measuring equipment which the most thorough magazines use nowadays. Its personnel quietly justify their attitude by saying that on the few occasions when they have relented, cars have not always returned in perfect condition. The attitude is perhaps understandable, and almost seems to work in Ferrari's favour. Its cars are placed on such a lofty pedestal that the Ferrari legend intensifies.

AN EXQUISITE OPPORTUNITY
A Ferrari driving day

Just occasionally, however, there is a chink of light in the iron curtain for the privileged journalists who have been lucky enough to drive every exotic car *except* a Ferrari. One such chance came one day in Oxfordshire in 1986 when Maranello Concessionaires Ltd assembled examples of the four models in its range. Alongside a scarlet Testarossa – attracting all the attention – were a 328GTB, a 412i and a 328 Mondial. As if to emphasise the weight of the occasion, even Stirling Moss was there to examine the current products of the company for which he had been due to drive before his 1962 accident halted his racing career.

It was a sublime day, based as we were at one of England's great restaurants, Le Manoir aux Quat' Saisons at Great Milton. The sun was beating down and the scent of freshly mown grass hung in the air. A morning driving these great glories of Italy was to be followed by chef Raymond Blanc's world-famous cuisine. It would have needed only Sophia Loren's presence to make it the most perfect day imaginable.

This was the first time I drove a Testarossa, but another opportunity came later with a car borrowed for a day from Town & Country, an English car

rental firm based in London which has grown partly through specialising in supercars. Finally, during the course of our photographic and research visit to Maranello for this book, I had the memorable experience of a few laps round Fiorano alongside chief test driver Giorgio Enrico. It was captivating to watch his relaxed, fluid control as he hustled a left-hand drive Testarossa around the circuit. I am certain he was driving well within his capabilities, but our tyre-squealing laps were awe-inspiring nonetheless.

GETTING TO KNOW THE CAR
First sensations

Tucking your fingers underneath the top of the gaping air vent curving inwards along the Testarossa's flanks finds the door handle, which you squeeze towards you to open the door. Although the door swings open wide, clambering into the driver's seat needs some agility because the cabin is so low and the windscreen pillar rakes back at such a shallow angle. You have to step over the sill, grasp the pillar to stop yourself toppling

over and ease yourself down into the seat. Once installed, you sit so low that you are almost level with the road.

Although many Italian cars of the past, Ferraris included, have been cursed with appalling driving positions suitable only for gorilla-shaped people with short legs and long arms, finding the ideal combination of seat and steering wheel position is possible in the Testarossa. Raising a bar under your knees moves the seat back and fore, and three little switches – more easily reached with the door open – control other seat movements electrically. You can alter the backrest angle, move the backrest back and fore, and raise the seat cushion. Slippery leather does not seem the ideal surface to anchor you into these seats, but they do have large side sections to brace your body against high cornering forces. The head restraint, a large flat pad, can also be moved up and down by hand.

The steering wheel does not adjust telescopically, but can be raised or lowered to suit your height. With all these adjustments set to fit your shape, you sit with your legs angled slightly towards the centre of the car, your feet tucked to the left of the front wheelarch intrusion which supports a large loudspeaker. The pedals are chunky, with the large pads for clutch and brake hinged from above and the long accelerator extending down to pivot from the floor. They are quite close together so that you can comfortably work the accelerator with your heel as you toe the brake.

TESTAROSSA FAMILIARISATION
Settling into the driver's seat

This steering wheel sits nicely in your fingers, its diameter and rim width perfect for the fluent hand movement which high-speed driving requires. Its three alloy spokes, painted in silk-finish black, are ideally placed so that your thumbs cradle the two upper spokes with your hands on the leather rim at the ten-to-two position. Unlike the modern vogue for placing the horn at the end of a column stalk, the Testarossa has its horn push where you can find it in a hurry – in the centre of the steering wheel. Naturally the horn boss is a yellow disc

bearing a Prancing Horse, and surrounding it are the six flush Allen bolts that secure the wheel to the steering column.

Ahead of you through the windscreen, which rakes back to finish close to your forehead, can be seen only scenery, for the Testarossa's nose drops so low that it is invisible from inside – you could be sitting at the very front of the car. Visibility from the driving seat, however, is remarkably good for such a low mid-engined machine, and much better than a Lamborghini Countach or Lotus Esprit. Thin windscreen pillars and unobtrusive quarter-light bars allow an excellent view ahead and to the sides. The two exterior mirrors show some of the rear wings as well as plenty of the road itself, while the internal mirror gives a reasonable rearwards view framed by the roof and the red bulge of the engine cover. Where mid-engined cars often prove difficult to manage in traffic is in rear three-quarter vision, but if you turn your head in the Testarossa the fixed side windows which blend into the body panel buttresses afford an excellent view. Unlike many mid-engined cars, the Testarossa promotes no feelings of claustrophobia, its generous glass area and pale upholstery making the interior pleasantly airy.

The two most important instruments, speedometer and tachometer, face you through the top of the steering wheel. Their markings are picked out in aggressive orange, which looks purposeful but is harder to read than conventional white on black. With so many increments to fit on a dial reading up to 200mph, calibration has to be limited to a stroke marking every 10mph and a figure for every 20mph – at the British speed limit the needle is only a third of the way round its arc! One minor criticism is the way the hood around the instrument panel reflects in the windscreen in sunlight. As on a current GTO or a Daytona, a matt suede finish (instead of shiny brown leather) along the top of the fascia would easily solve this, and avoid distracting images in your field of vision.

In all other respects, the Testarossa's interior could almost belong to any other more mundane car, stylish though it is in design. There are three steering column stalks (Fiat owners would recognise their origin) for the usual functions – lights, indicators and wipers – and a range of clearly marked switches along the centre console. The fly-off handbrake has an unusual position, behind the seat and the door, but otherwise has a conventional ratchet hold. Like a Jaguar's, it lies flush with the floor whether on or off so that you do not catch your trouser leg as you climb into the car. On the other hand, it is so difficult to slide your hand down between seat and door trim to reach the handle that you tend not to use it.

The gearlever is perfectly positioned where your left hand drops naturally from the steering wheel. Its chromed stick, topped by a simple black sphere the size of a golf ball, sprouts almost vertically from the aperture at its root, and then bends towards you. The lever sits within a cut-out on the passenger's side of the centre console – its position is ideal for right-hand drive, but perhaps a little close to the driver on a left-hand drive car. By now, fully familiar with the environment around you, you ease the gearlever gently through its six positions to get the feel of its action. It is firm to use compared with most modern cars, but tremen-

dously precise as you crank it through its slots, enjoying the evocative clicks – a constant reminder that you're in a Ferrari – as the lever knocks against its gate.

Like many performance cars with ZF gearboxes, the Testarossa has a shift pattern which starts with a dog-leg first away from you and back. Second to fifth are followed in sequence in the normal way, with fifth placed near you and back. Reverse is opposite first. Familiarisation is worthwhile, for in the heat of the moment you may need to remember in a hurry that each ratio is opposite the position found in most cars. Ferrari has it right, however, in placing first gear out on a limb, for it is rarely used when you drive a Testarossa in its natural habitat. Most of the time you are stirring between fourth and fifth, which is a slick push or pull through a single plane instead of an awkward movement through neutral across two planes.

THE WORLD'S FINEST ENGINE
Flexibility and power

You could be in almost any modern fuel-injected car as you start the engine, by turning the key on the right-hand side of the steering column. With fuel injection there is no choke, and the routine of so many past Ferraris – depressing the throttle fully a couple of times to prime the Weber carburettors – seems long gone. You just gently tickle the accelerator pedal when you hear the big flat-12 catch, and suddenly the whole car vibrates, trembling slightly from side to side in sympathy with the joyous whoop behind your ears. Settling back to tickover, a restrained growling sound full of the promise of immense power mumbles away 2ft behind your head.

Despite being aware of how strenuously Ferrari worked during the process of refining Berlinetta Boxer into Testarossa, my very first impression of this supercar is of how gently all the controls operate. The clutch is especially sweet, with such a light, syrupy motion that you pull slowly away, caressing the revs up to 2000rpm, having not even noticed it. Straight away this is an indication of what is in store, for the Boxer – in common with many other supercars, such as the Porsche 911 Turbo – had such a sharp clutch that it was easy to

stall the car first time. The Boxer's left pedal was also so heavy that it became wearing on long journeys through traffic, but the Testarossa has removed this shortcoming. The steering, too, is light enough not to tax your biceps as you make your first manoeuvres. The narrower front tyres and relatively small proportion of weight over the front wheels help here, but at parking speeds you could believe that the rack and pinion system is power-assisted.

The sensations that will last with you forever soon make themselves felt on the open road, and it is the flat-12's astonishing combination of flexibility and power which makes the strongest impression. Quite simply, this is one of the finest engines the world has ever seen, with four times the power of an average family saloon. It spins up to its 6800rpm red line with sewing machine smoothness, emitting a depth of symphonic sound which can come only from twelve large cylinders pumping away in perfect harmony. Older Ferrari V12s give the same feeling of inner strength, but the whine of their valve gear and camshaft drive have been all but ironed out of the flat-12 to leave a wonderfully pure, deep-chested roar which rises in pitch to a baritone cry towards peak revs. But for the absence of spitting and crackling from the exhaust, this could be a fully-fledged racing engine.

In its responses, however, this is no temperamental competition unit. You might expect the flat-12 to feel cammy and peaky in the traditional style of performance engines, but as the engine climbs its scale at no point do you perceive any feeling of fireworks suddenly beginning, as if the touchpaper has been lit. Instead, the flat-12 delivers its punch in one progressive, fluid surge of power, all the way from 1000rpm to 6800rpm. There is no decisive 'right-let's-get-going' stab in the back, just the insistent push of an engine that works for you all the time, pressing forwards like a giant hand.

On the open road in the Appennine foothills, *below*. In all conditions the Testarossa feels remarkably light to drive, although its bulk, *right*, is clearly seen in views from front and rear.

In any gear, the feeling of being assailed by a mighty, continuous force is always present, seducing you to press hard on the throttle at every opportunity. The engine is too eager to be held back on the leash; it wants to perform for you all the time, whether it is catapulting the car forwards from 15mph to 75mph in second or from 25mph to 135mph in fourth. It can stretch itself over incredible speed bands in any gear, all the way up to 180mph in fifth if there is ever an opportunity to experience it. It is rewarding to slot the lever around the gearbox to experience the engine's intoxicating wail, but the Testarossa is so docile that you do not have to drive like this to make the most of its shattering performance. It will break the British speed limit shortly after you change out of first if you indulge in full-blooded starts, yet it is tractable enough in fifth to pull unhesitatingly, with no hint of driveline 'shunt', from a whisker over 1000rpm, or just 30mph. Imagine it: from 30mph to 180mph in one long, relentless climb.

STUNNING ACCELERATION
The ever-eager engine

The breadth of the Testarossa's acceleration is staggering, for the power flows so smoothly and strongly. This is best illustrated by quoting *Motor*'s figures for fourth gear acceleration over 20mph increments (60–80mph, 70–90mph and so on). Starting at 20–40mph, the times for each successive band are 4.5sec, 4.4sec, 4.4sec, 4.5sec, 4.6sec, 4.7sec, 4.9sec, 5.7sec and 6.7sec – and this last figure is for 100–120mph. So smooth and sustained is the flat-12's lusty pull that it actually does not feel subjectively as fast as a cammier engine which kicks you more dramatically up the road. This flexibility is the Testarossa's greatest asset in day-to-day driving, even if it removes just a touch of the tingle from its acceleration.

Although other supercars can better some of the Testarossa's figures, none can produce such consistent acceleration, regardless of speed. They all have great engines, but the Testarossa's flat-12 is the best for its combination of outright power and fulsome torque. Distilling available performance figures shows that the Testarossa is roughly on a par with machines such as the Aston Martin Vantage or Porsche 911 Turbo for through-the-gears standing start times up to 120mph, but thereafter it pulls out an advantage which it maintains all the way to its higher top speed. Even the Lamborghini Countach *quattrovalvole*, a leaner car which comfortably beats the Testarossa's 0–100km (62.1mph) time of 5.8sec by dipping into the rarefied sub-5sec bracket, cannot quite exceed its Maranello rival's 180mph maximum speed.

Many a supercar needs well-chosen gearbox ratios to complement the power characteristics of its engine, but the Testarossa's flat-12 is so tireless that it could compensate for the most irregular ratios. Although a hard change from first to fifth reveals that the gears are stepped in good proportion, the question is almost academic. It has a gearbox, and that is all you need to know. The gearlever always needs a firm grasp to take the changes; its solid action is precise, if not particularly slick. Changes cannot be hurried through terribly quickly, especially when threading the lever across the planes (from first to second or third to fourth), but the most important movement of all, fourth to fifth and vice versa, can be made very swiftly. And through these processes the clutch is so gentle and forgiving – but unquestionably strong – that a mistimed change never results in a snatch as the drive takes up again.

HANDLING APPROACHING PERFECTION
More rubber on the road

In the way it handles, the Testarossa marks a great advance over the Boxer, even if it is a shade softer. Mid-engined cars have a reputation for sailing undramatically round corners at incredible speed at up to, say, 90 per cent effort, but squeezing that last 10 per cent can get you in all sorts of trouble. They generally corner with a fairly neutral balance which keeps its composure admirably until the sudden snap into a spin. Both the Boxer and the Testarossa, however, have a rearwards weight bias which makes them depart slightly from this pattern, although they differ significantly in handling character.

Where the Testarossa steps ahead of the Boxer is in how well controlled its rear end remains when you are pushing hard. For all the Boxer's tenacious grip and formidable cornering ability, you could never quite forget that it had a great weight in its tail which could begin to act like a pendulum. When the back did start to nudge out of line, perhaps over sudden bumps, you felt that you needed to call upon every reserve of your skill and reflexes to catch it quickly before the dramas compounded themselves. It was both a rewarding and demanding car to drive quickly, but your faith in it was never quite total.

You suspect that Ferrari's work on the Testarossa's suspension was aimed at alleviating this hint of insecurity, for the newer car immediately inspires more confidence. For a start, its 255 section rear tyres plant 30mm more rubber on the road than the Boxer ever did, and the difference is marked at all times. You notice the terrific traction by the reluctance of the tyres to

Brutal treatment in first gear – this is test driver Giorgio Enrico on Fiorano's steering pad, *left* – will push the tail sideways. Otherwise the car corners with great poise and is stable in a straight line, as shown *below*

break grip from a standing start or when powering through slow corners in a low gear. Being brutal through a hairpin, of course, will send the Testarossa's tail slithering sideways, but the breakdown of grip is comfortably controllable by quickly unwinding the steering to apply opposite lock. The car displays a fluid progression towards restrained oversteer which requires no great skill to enjoy.

This is provocative driving, the sort of thing you do on an empty road at slow speeds. In all normal circumstances, the Testarossa corners with delicious composure, turning in crisply and taking its chosen line cleanly as you increase pressure on the throttle. You feel just a suggestion of stabilising understeer through the steering, and this gives safe warning if you press too hard. If the tugging from the front wheels builds up to the point where you might run too close to the edge of the road, you can lift off a fraction with no sense of upsetting the tail. The rear wheels stay glued to their path, and the nose slightly tightens into the corner once more.

The grip is so great that these characteristics are barely perceptible, but they make the Testarossa a safe car to handle. Unlike the Boxer, you never have the disquieting feeling that something unpredictable is about to occur. If you stamp suddenly on the throttle at high cornering speeds, the rear wheels just push the car a little more insistently towards understeer, and lifting off sharply brings it gently back to line. This subtle and safe understeering tendency, accompanied by a little more roll than the Boxer exhibited, could detract from the Testarossa's appeal for some expert drivers, but it is typical of the direction in which modern supercars – which sell, after all, to owners with money but not necessarily immense skill – are heading. It is a car which you can trust to corner at great speed with total security.

Only in one respect is the handling of the Testarossa at all disappointing, and that is in comparison with one of its sisters, the 328GTB,

probably the finest handling car in the world. Against this agile, pure-bred sports car, the Testarossa can feel a little unwieldy, and just too big for the road. But this is a criticism which bears weight only when measuring it against the best, for the 328GTB fits around its driver like a second skin – you and the car become a single entity working in perfect harmony.

If you feel just occasionally that the Testarossa has marginally softer handling responses than the Boxer, the pay-off comes in the ride. This is outstanding by any standards, let alone for a 180mph supercar. Ferrari's mid-engined cars, right back to the Dino 246 of the 1960s, have always been very comfortable to travel in, and the Testarossa is the best yet. Road ripples, lumps and potholes are handled with a composure that is hard to square with its handling crispness – the compromise is always elusive, although Lotus are past masters at it. Springing is sufficiently compliant for the wheels to hop delicately over bumps, and the damping powerfully forces them back down again. The suspension engineering is just right for a car intended to combine sports and grand touring character – you feel the bumps, but you are not jarred by them.

FINGER-LIGHT STEERING
Testarossa has no power assistance

Since the Testarossa's steering feels comfortable when manoeuvring, it is no surprise that it becomes almost finger-light at speed. You never have to grip the wheel tightly, instead caressing it gently with palms and fingertips to keep its liveliness under control. Its ratio of nearly three and a half turns from lock to lock is just right to avoid over-sensitive response to your movements, but still you must be delicate with it, so instantly does the car dart to your command. At high speed it is perhaps a shade too sensitive to track effortlessly in a straight line, but the car never feels unstable as you make tiny corrective movements.

The Testarossa's brakes are one of its strongest

Testarossa looks blatantly aggressive from this angle, but it is an unusually refined supercar. Excellent suppression of wind and tyre noise, a compliant ride and a comfortable interior combine to make it an effortless high-performance car over long distances.

features, and once again they have been lightened up compared with the Boxer's. Their specification, a quartet of huge ventilated discs, is similar, but four-pot calipers provide even more gripping power. The servo assistance is really quite noticeable, with a light pedal pressure which can cause you to lock up in an emergency, but the brakes are comfortable and easy to use once you have adapted. They pull up the car – no lightweight

at over a ton and half unladen – brilliantly and repeatedly, with no sign of fade. ABS has taken a long time to arrive at Ferrari, and it must be said that in today's market the Testarossa is incomplete without it.

This lightness of control which manifests itself in every facet of the Testarossa's character helps to make it a much more refined car, and perhaps a less overtly sporting one, than the Boxer. But all the detailed attention lavished on the Testarossa during its development – including its superior luggage space – has turned it into a far better machine for long journeys. It is never tiring or stressful to drive, and you can easily envisage covering vast distances in one hop. A thousand miles in a day on the right roads (and in the right countries) would be an exhilarating experience.

The engine's sonorous growl is always the major sound in the cabin, but it never becomes overwhelming. Although it changes in pitch and tenor as it builds to a high-revving crescendo, it is not an unwelcome intrusion, just a key part of the car's soul. Against this, all the other sources of noise pale away to insignificance. Wind roar around the door mirrors and tyre rumble are to be expected, but these sounds are kept well in check below 100mph. As you would expect from a car of this quality, there are no rattles or squeaks from the interior fittings over bumpy roads.

Only one thing detracts from the ease of driving a Testarossa, and that is the car's immense width. Down narrower B roads and country lanes it is distinctly unnerving to have to worry about whether you are going to clout anything with the

rear wings. Whether pointing the car through a gap, passing a parked car in town or just reversing into a parking space, you mentally allow an extra 6in. because the rear of the car is appreciably wider than the cockpit in which you sit. Although the Testarossa seems to shrink around you as you get to know it, the width – it is 17in. broader than a Fiat Uno, for heaven's sake! – is its most intimidating feature at first, and many miles later it remains uppermost in your mind when driving through towns.

By contrast, it is far easier to make allowances for the height of the car, because so many other supercars are just as low slung. You become used to the difficulties of peering round vehicles in front of you, but you know that when you can see to overtake you are in the oncoming lane for the

briefest period. The door mirrors of current cars are thoroughly practical and steady at speed, but a severe drawback of the earlier high-mounted single mirror was that it completely obscured your view to the right as you entered a roundabout.

A REFINED SUPERCAR
Marrying sophistication and performance

While its excellent suppression of noise makes the Testarossa a refined car, its interior equipment is comprehensive enough to build this impression still further. As well as expected features like electric operation for windows, mirrors, seats and door locking, there is a superb air conditioning system. The 'goldfish bowl' effect of the Testarossa's large windscreen makes good ventilation essential on hot days, but its air

conditioning is up to the job. It has infinitely variable temperature and fan speed settings, and parallels Rolls-Royce's sophistication in providing separate controls for driver and passenger.

If you expect a supercar to be a raw-edged machine built for just one purpose – to travel as fast as possible with no concession to creature comfort – you might be a trifle disappointed by the Testarossa's refinement. It is not quite the quickest accelerating or most agile cornering of 1980s supercars, but it is the most rounded in its capabilities. As roads become busier and speed limits restrict most of Europe to less than half the Testarossa's maximum, supercars need to become grand tourers as well as thoroughbred sporting machines. The Testarossa is absolutely in tune with its time.

INDEX

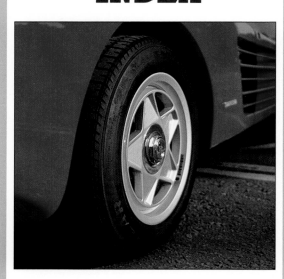

Note: Page numbers in italics refer to illustrations

A

ABS *see* Automatic Braking System
air conditioning 20, 22, 37, 63
Assembly *see* Engine assembly; final assembly
Automatic Braking System 22, 62

B

Bazzi, Luigi 5
Behra, Jean *12–13*
Bellei, Dr Ing. Angelo 14
Berlinetta Boxer *see* Ferrari 365GT4 BB; 512BB
Berlinetta Lusso *see* Ferrari 250GT
Body *20*, 30, 40, *44*
Boxer *see* Ferrari 365GT4 BB; 512BB
Brakes 18, 22, 28, 39, 61–2

C

Cambiano (Pininfarina centre) 15, *15*, 53
Chassis 30, 40
Chiti, Ing. Carlo 11,12
Collins, Peter 12
Colombo, Gioacchino 5
Commission Sportive Internationale 11
Cooling *see* Radiators
CSI *see* Commission Sportive Internationale

D

Daytona *see* Ferrari 365GTB/4
de Angelis, Dr Ing Giuliano 16
Donington *6–7*
Driving impressions 54–63

E

Engine 17–18, 24–5, 38, 46, 56
assembly 50, *50*, 51, *51*
see also flat-12 engine; V12 engine
Enrico, Giorgio 22, 54, *60*, 61

F

Fantuzzi, Medardo 12
Farina, Battista (Pinin) 53; *see also* Pininfarina
Ferrari cars:
250GT (including Berlinetta Lusso) 5–6
275GTB *4–5*, 6, *6*
365GTB/4 (Daytona) 6, *6–7*, 7–9
365GT4 BB (Berlinetta Boxer) *7*, 8–10, 14
512BB (Berlinetta Boxer) *10*, 14, 18, 20, 22, 24
GTO 3, *8–9*
see also Testa Rossa; Testarossa
company history 4–5, 52–3
Ferrari, Enzo 4–5, 14, 52–3
Fiat buy-in 52
Final assembly 44, *45*
Finishing 51
Fiorano (test track) *20*, *21*, 22, *60*, 61
Fioravanti, Leonardo 15–16
Flat-12 engine *7*, 8–10, 16, 24, 46, 56, 58
Flexible Manufacturing System (FMS) 48, *48*
Forghieri, Ing. Mauro 16
Foundry 46, *46*, *47*
Four-valve technology 17–18, 24
Fraschetti, Ing. Andrea 11
Fuel consumption 39
Fuel ignition 10, 14, 18, 24–5, 38, 56

G

Gears 27, 39, 56
Gendebien, Olivier 11–13
Grugliasco (Pininfarina plant) 16, *22*, 40–41, *41* *42*, *42–3*, *44*, 53

H

Hawthorn, Mike 12
Hill, Phil 12–13

I

Ignition 24, 39
Instrumentation 34, 56
Interior 34
ITCA 16, 40

L

Lampredi, Aurelio 5
Le Mans 8, 11–13
Lighting 32
Lubrication 24, 39
Lusso *see* Ferrari 250GT

M

Machining 48, *48*
Manufacture 40–52
Maranello (Ferrari works) 16, 40, 44, 45–6, *46*, *47*, *47*, 48, *48*, 52
Maranello Concessionaires Ltd 54
Materazzi, Ing. Nicola 14, 16
Mid-engined configuration *7*, 8–9, 61
Modena 52

N

Nardo (test track) 22–3
Noise level 20, 62–3
Nürburgring 11–13

P

Painting 40–41, *41*, *42*, 51

G *(continued)*

Performance 39
Pininfarina 5–7, 9, 12, 15, 30, 53
Styling *16–17*, *18–19*, *20*
see also Cambiano; Grugliasco

R

Radiators 14, 22, 24, 30, 38
Razelli, Giovanni 52
Rossi, Ing. Maurizio *14*; *quoted* 14, 15, 18, 22, 23

S

Scaglietti, Sergio 5, 6, 11–12, 52
Sebring *12*, 13
Sguazzini, Ing. Giovanni 52
Specifications 38–9
Steering 27, 39, 55, 61
Studi e Ricerche (Pininfarina) *see* Cambiano
Styling *see* Pininfarina
Supercar heritage 3–5
Suspension 6, 8, 27, 39, 61

T

Targa Florio 12–13
Testa Rossa 11, *11*, 12, *12–13*, 13
Testarossa: origins 14
Transmission 27, 39
Trim 34, 40–42, *43*
Tyres 28, 39

V

V12 engine 4–5, 7–8, 11

W

Wheels 28, 39
World Sports Car Championships 11–13

Z

Zincrox 40

PICTURE CREDITS
The publishers wish to thank the following photographers and organisations who have supplied photographs for this book:

Author: 5, 6, 7, 8–9, 10, 11, 12–13

John Conway: back cover, title page, 4 (left), 34, 38, 64.
Industrie Pininfarina S.p.A: 22, 23

All other photographs in this book, including endpapers and front cover, were taken by **Jim Forrest**